What Readers Are Saying About
Land the Tech Job You Love

Andy Lester has done what no one has ever been able to do. He has written a software manual that teaches techies how to land a great job. Done up with style and insight that speaks clearly to programmers and other technical folks, this how-to guide shows you how to design, code, debug, and run a successful job-hunting project.

► **Nick Corcodilos**
  asktheheadhunter.com

The timing couldn't be better for Andy Lester's fantastic new book, *Land the Tech Job You Love*. In these difficult economic times, a lot more people are competing for a lot fewer jobs, and they're going to need all the help they can get. Andy's excellent collection of guidelines and pragmatic advice may be the bible we all depend upon.

► **Ed Yourdon**
  Author of *Death March* and developer of software methodologies

A perceptive, practical, positive, and powerful guide to scoring your next great tech job.

► **Karen Burns**
  Author, *The Amazing Adventures of Working Girl:*
  Real-Life Career Advice You Can Actually Use

The people who have *always* stood out to me in interviews were not always the most talented candidates but the most prepared. This book will give you the tools, tips, and real-world experience that are invaluable to getting hired. If you are going to pick up one book on getting hired, this is the one you need.

► **Jason A. Crome**
  Partner, DEVNET, Inc.

This is a valuable, readable book that cuts through the normal B.S. of job hunting. If you ever think you will need a job, do yourself a favor and buy a copy of this book now.

► **Johanna Rothman**
  Author and management consultant

Land the Tech Job You Love is one part sound advice, one part self-psychoanalysis, and one part wincing as you recognize things you've personally done. I wish I'd had this years ago.

► **Dee Ann LeBlanc**
  Technical writer, Renaissoft

You don't have to be unemployed to benefit from reading (studying!) this book. It's a great book to read *before* you start looking. Andy thoroughly analyzes the many issues involved in the complex process of finding the job you will love.

► **Ilya Talman**
  President, Roy Talman & Associates

Andy has taken the mystery and guesswork out of the technology career change. Essential stuff.

► **Rob Warmowski**
  Principal, South Loop Digital

Land the Tech Job You Love

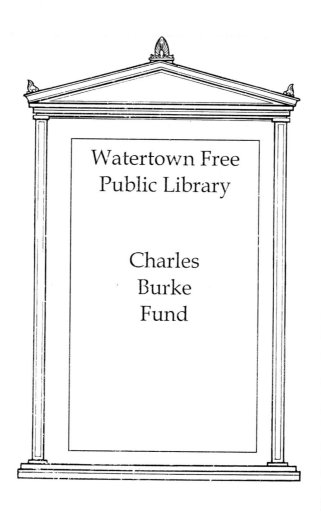

Land the Tech Job You Love

Andy Lester

The Pragmatic Bookshelf
Raleigh, North Carolina   Dallas, Texas

Pragmatic Bookshelf

Many of the designations used by manufacturers and sellers to distinguish their products are claimed as trademarks. Where those designations appear in this book, and The Pragmatic Programmers, LLC was aware of a trademark claim, the designations have been printed in initial capital letters or in all capitals. The Pragmatic Starter Kit, The Pragmatic Programmer, Pragmatic Programming, Pragmatic Bookshelf and the linking *g* device are trademarks of The Pragmatic Programmers, LLC.

Every precaution was taken in the preparation of this book. However, the publisher assumes no responsibility for errors or omissions, or for damages that may result from the use of information (including program listings) contained herein.

Our Pragmatic courses, workshops, and other products can help you and your team create better software and have more fun. For more information, as well as the latest Pragmatic titles, please visit us at

http://www.pragprog.com

ISBN-10: 1-934356-26-3
ISBN-13: 978-1-934356-26-5
Printed on acid-free paper.
P1.0 printing, May 2009
Version: 2009-5-19

Contents

Appreciations

In *Behind Closed Doors* [RD05], Johanna Rothman discusses what she calls *appreciations*, simple but powerful messages to let people know how they have affected your life. They take this form: "[Person], I appreciate you for [something]. Its effect on me was [whatever]." They're a fantastic way to let people know just what they mean to you, and to build relationships, both in business and personal life.

I've titled this section "Appreciations," instead of the usual "Acknowledgments," because *acknowledgments* is not strong enough a word. Acknowledging someone sounds like rote, mundane, minimal. You acknowledge you were informed of your Miranda rights.

Herein I'd like to let some very important people know just how much I appreciate their assistance, guidance, and support in bringing this book to you, the reader. If you like this book and you happen to meet or know one of them, please add your voice to mine and share your appreciation.

Bill Odom, I appreciate how much common ground we shared when we first talked about the problems of hiring quality people. If it had not been for that germ of an idea to teach the process of getting a job or our first conference presentation, this book would not exist.

Seth Gumble, Kristen Henmueller, Adrian Howard, Pete Krawczyk, Phil Morrison, Johanna Rothman, Ricardo Signes, and Kate Thieda, who all contributed stories, I appreciate your unique additions to the book. From the first day I thought of writing a book, I knew it had to have real stories, both good and bad, to illustrate how best to find a job and also for a little levity. This book is all the richer for your tales.

Johanna Rothman, I appreciate your criticism and ideas and having you as a cheerleader every day. Early in the formation of this book, you sent an email saying "I'm rooting for you! WRITE THAT BOOK!" I never told you this, but I copied that into the book source file, a constant reminder of support when I sometimes (often?) didn't feel like writing.

Pete Krawczyk, I appreciate your constant support and contribution to this effort. Every forwarded blog posting, every suggestion, and every idea of another nugget to add to this book has helped improve what you now hold in your hands.

To my reviewers, Tony Bianchi, Karen Burns, Clarke Ching, Jason Crome, Selena Deckelmann, Esther Derby, Paul Fenwick, Zack Grossbart, Kim Gloff, Adrian Howard, Erika Jones, Pete Krawczyk, Dan Lester, Gabrielle Roth, Johanna Rothman, Ricardo Signes, Graeme Thomas, Rob Warmowski, and everyone on the Pragmatic Job Hunting mailing list at the beginning of this project, I appreciate the wealth of insights, corrections, comments, and suggestions from each of you. Your positive comments and encouragement in the early stages helped give us all the confidence that we were on the right track.

Susannah Davidson Pfalzer, my cruel but fair editor, I appreciate your guidance throughout the process of writing the book and your patience when things took longer than either of us would've liked. If not for you, this book would still be just an ever-expanding ~/job-book/ideas.txt file.

Daniel Steinberg, I appreciate your feedback as I brought this book home and for helming the new Pragmatic Life series. My book is better because of your perceptive notes, and I hope that my work here helps build a foundation for future titles with the Pragmatic touch.

Andy Hunt and Dave Thomas, I'm grateful for your faith in me, giving a fledgling author a chance based on little more than some presentation slides and a half-hour chat on the phone. I also appreciate what a marvelous process for creating books you've created for Pragmatic authors. It has eliminated the painful mechanics of book creation, leaving only the painful writing.

Allison Randal, I appreciate having a wise book editor who is always willing to lend an eye to a problem. You have helped me break through mental dams, providing new perspectives and ideas on problems that stymied me and Susannah because we were simply too close to the material.

Kim Gloff and Joy Williams, I appreciate your work on the development of the icons that we planned to use in the book, especially Kim for creating them. Although we eventually decided to use only one of the icons, going through the process with you helped me identify the themes on which I wanted to focus.

Nick Corcodilos, I'm grateful for *Ask the Headhunter* [Cor97], the book that made me rethink everything I knew about the job search process. It helped me as a manager when hiring, and it provided inspiration to write this book. I'm also thankful for your pointed analysis of the CareerBuilder mission statement, which gave me powerful evidence to help steer job hunters away from the swamp of the job boards.

Seth Gumble and Debbie Schober, I appreciate your guidance in my formative years of management and believing that this programmer could make the transition to leader. Your patient instruction—and swift, firm corrections when necessary—improved me, taught me all about the hiring process, and so improved this book.

Damian Conway, I have always appreciated your genius at programming and your inspiration as a speaker, but here I want to appreciate how gracious a person you are. When I read your thanks to me in the acknowledgments for *Perl Best Practices* [Con05], I'd never felt so honored. I thought, "If I ever get to write a book, I'm going to do my acknowledgments like that." I hope the others named here feel as honored as I did.

Carol Rios, I appreciate how you let me set up shop for hours at a time at my second office, Tacos El Norte in McHenry. I wrote probably half of the book at table #5 in your fine establishment.

Most of all, to my wife and best friend, Amy, and my daughter and Rock Band 2 band member, Quinn, I appreciate your daily love and support and for making the nongeek parts of my life so joyous. Amy, for all the times you took care of parenting and housework when I was hunched over my laptop and for all the times you urged me on when I said "I don't even feel like finishing the thing," this book is for you.

Introduction

This book is about your happiness.

You spend half your waking hours at your job. That's more time than you spend with your kids or your spouse and even more than time spent playing World of Warcraft. You can't be happy with your life when you're spending so much time doing something you don't love.

This book is here first to help you be happy with your life by helping you understand what you want in a job and then to help you find and land that job. My goal in writing this book is to help you find a job that you love as much as Ed Coughlin loved his.

The Fireman Who Loved His Job

Ed Coughlin loved his job. He was a fireman for the city of Chicago for twenty-eight years and loved every minute of it. It's certainly not something that everyone is cut out for, but he excelled at it, making the rank of captain. After retiring from the Chicago Fire Department to the suburbs, he couldn't leave the life. He was a volunteer fireman for a number of small towns in the area and never lost touch with the friends he made.

In the too-short time that I knew Ed in his fading years, nothing would bring a glint to his eye like recalling the time he spent as a fireman. He'd tell stories of the fire calls as if they'd happened yesterday and have everyone laughing with the tales of firehouse antics. I know it was important to him that he made a difference in countless lives, but I think that even more than that he just loved the work, loved the people, and loved *being a fireman*.

Many of us in the tech fields are like Ed the fireman. Whether programmer, system administrator, web designer, or some other technical specialist, we live similar lives. We have jobs that many others would never want to do, and yet we thrive at them. Those we serve are often highly appreciative. Our subculture is tightly knit but misunderstood by the outside world. Most of all, we love the work we do so much we sometimes volunteer to do it just so that we can do more. Many of us see being professional geeks as a calling—what we were meant to do. It's just what we *are*.

How This Book Was Born

This book started on January 14, 2004, after a Perl Mongers meeting in St. Louis, Missouri.[1] After the meeting, twenty of us made our way to dinner. We sat at a long table, about ten geeks to a side. Across from me sat fellow techie Bill Odom, and we got to discussing the trouble we were having hiring qualified people for our respective companies. We traded stories of bad résumés and bad interviews. Someone asked for advice on how he could do better on his résumé. Then someone else asked how he could tell whether he should leave his job. Within ten minutes, we had the entire table clustered around us, interested in job issues. Bill said, "We ought to take our act on the road."

Later, Bill and I discussed how we'd tapped into something. People in the group were unhappy with their jobs and looking to change their situations. Conversely, Bill and I were dismayed by how many otherwise qualified candidates come through our offices screwing up their chances at getting something better. Worse, we had people who interviewed with us who had no idea whether the job for which they were applying was one they'd enjoy. They were setting themselves up for failure.

As I drove back home from St. Louis that night, Ed Coughlin, my wife's father and the fireman who loved his job so much, passed away. At the wake, dozens of friends from his years in fire protection paid their respects and shared their stories of how much Ed loved being a fireman.

---

1. Perl Mongers is the worldwide collection of Perl user groups. Visit http://www. pm.org to find one near you.

In the weeks following that meeting, Bill and I put together a talk for O'Reilly's Open Source Conference. It was a hit, and I gave the talk many times afterward at user groups around the country. The success of those talks led to this book.

My wish is for everyone to love their jobs as much as Ed loved his. I'm well on my way, having been a professional geek for more than twenty-one years, and I wouldn't trade it for anything else. I hope that you can find and keep the kind of happiness I get from my working life and that Ed got from his.

A Disclaimer of Sorts

Books of career advice can't be exactly about your situation. As the author, I don't know anything about you. I don't know your job situation, your history, your background, the type of job you're looking for, or what is important to you in life.

You'll have to adjust some advice to your given situation or your given location. If you live outside the United States, some advice may not apply. In some European countries, it's standard to include a photo with a résumé, where in the United States it's likely to get your résumé thrown away. Even within the United States, behavior at an interview in the Bay Area is likely to be very different from at a company in Chicago.

> Don't blindly follow the directions in a book.

And don't forget what I hear at least once every time I give a presentation about this topic: "I like how you approach this, but you're not like other managers! Most managers are clueless!"

So as the author, I don't know you, I don't know where you live, and the hiring process in many companies is fundamentally suboptimal.

And yet...

And yet, the principles apply. These techniques do work. The stories that illustrate the chapters underline the basic applicability of the ideas and practices.

And yet, I do know a bit about you, because I've talked to many technical professionals who are unhappy with their careers or working to move to a better place.

And yet, most of this book *does* apply to you. Most of the ideas are universal, crossing cultural boundaries. The guiding principles of matching yourself to the right job, of putting yourself in the shoes of the hiring manager, and of demonstrating your value to the interviewer all form a bedrock base from which your chances of getting a job and being happy with it are increased one-thousandfold.

Read this book, and the other books you read on getting hired, and consider how their advice apply to you. Take with you what makes sense, and leave the rest.

What's Inside?

This book is an interconnected network of ideas, all building on each other. The first two chapters lay the foundation of your search and your happiness. Chapter 1, *The Foundation of Your Job Search*, on page 3 discusses basic building blocks of how to be successful in the job hunt and in finding the job you want. The idea of "what you want" is so important, and so often ignored by hiring books, that it gets its own chapter, Chapter 2, *What Do You Want in a Job?*, on page 19. Even if you think you know what you're looking for in a job, you may be surprised at aspects of your working life you haven't considered.

The next two chapters discuss creating a stock résumé on which you'll base the custom résumés you send to companies. Résumé writing is a two-step process, so is discussed in two distinct chapters. The first—Chapter 3, *Résumé Content: Getting the Words Down*, on page 35—discusses only the words that you'll put on your résumés. This is to help steer you away from the temptation of making the résumé look good and giving the content inadequate attention. After you have the words down, you'll use the ideas in Chapter 4, *Building Your Résumé Documents*, on page 65 to build effective documents.

With a plan of what you want and a stock résumé, you can then look to finding a job, Chapter 5, *Finding Your Job*, on page 79.

Having found a job and company to pursue, you'll move on to Chapter 6, *Applying for the Job*, on page 109, finding the best way to make your introduction to the company.

Once you've been called in for an interview, your approach changes radically. You'll change from seeking a job to working to show the interviewer and company that you're the right person for the job and to find out for yourself that it's the right job for you. In Chapter 7, *Preparing for the Interview*, on page 123, you'll learn how to put together your plan and materials to make the run your way. Then, in Chapter 8, *The Interview*, on page 139, you'll learn how to work the interview and to make sure it's an opportunity to sell yourself as the best candidate, rather than a simple question-and-answer session.

The next two chapters discuss what to say, what not to say, and how best to say it. First, Chapter 9, *Handling the Tough Interview Questions*, on page 163 gives solid advice on how to answer those dreaded stumpers like "Where do you want to be in five years?" Then, Chapter 10, *Too Much Information*, on page 183 gives rules on what you should not say at an interview.

Chapter 11, *After the Interview: The Job Offer and Beyond*, on page 193 covers how to handle a job offer and how to make the most of a rejection. And, since your next job is probably not going to be your last, Chapter 12, *Staying Hirable*, on page 215 discusses how to make the most of your skills and career and how they're seen in the world so that the next time you need a job the process won't be so painful.

Finally, the appendixes give summaries of tips to make the most of your job hunt and present traps to avoid. You may want to skim them now to get a feel for what's coming up. Have a look at the inside front cover, too, for a list of rules to keep in mind during your job search.

Throughout the book, callouts give you important ideas to remember as your move forward. You'll also see this icon of an *F* on a report card. These mark potential failure points in the process. Don't repeat these mistakes others have made.

Land the Tech Job You Love Online

Follow up your reading of the book by participating online. The home page for the book is online at http://www.pragprog.com/titles/algh/land-the-tech-job-you-love. You can submit errata from that page, and you can also participate in the *Land The Tech Job You Love* forum at http://forums.pragprog.com/forums/81.

I welcome your comments, suggestions, and stories about hiring, either in the book forum or privately in email. I'd love to know whether this book helped you and how I could have done better.

Go Love Your Job

I know that many of you may be incredulous at the idea of loving your job. Maybe you liked working with computers, but your job has sucked the fun out. Your artistic side isn't satisfied designing boring websites. Your co-workers are obnoxious boors you dread. I know the feeling. You're not alone.

Life is too short for a job you don't love.
You're not stuck. Other opportunities are available for you, if you know where to look and can work the hiring process to your advantage and to the advantage of the company that hires you.

This book will help you get that job you love.

Andy Lester
May 2009
andy@theworkinggeek.com

Part I

The Job Search

Chapter 1

The Foundation of Your Job Search

A few basic principles should underlie your job search and carry over into all aspects of your career:

- Be honest with yourself.

- Be honest with others.

- Think like the boss.

- Be a problem solver.

- Sell yourself.

- Tell stories.

- Be positive.

These fundamentals interrelate and build on each other throughout the rest of the book and your job search. You'll need to sell yourself as a problem solver, because you know that's what the boss wants, and you'll do it by telling stories.

1.1 Be Honest with Yourself

There's no better way to wind up in an unhappy situation than to lie to yourself. What are your needs? What are your skills? What do you want in a job? What do you want to avoid? What really matters? Do you really need a given salary? How much time can you spend commuting, away from your spouse and kids? Can you actually do the job you have your eye set on? It's easy to fool yourself into accepting false answers when you're itching to get a new job. Far too many people wind up in ill-fitting jobs they hate because they've lied to themselves about what was important and what they could do.

Lying up front won't change the reality of your situation when you finally get started at that new job. If you really hate working with Java, convincing yourself that maybe it's not so bad isn't going to help you when you're up to your elbows in it a month into the new gig. If you're not actually a Java expert and you've fooled your boss into hiring you based on that premise, the outcome isn't going to be pleasant.

Over the years I've had dozens of conversations with people asking for advice about their careers or whether a certain job sounds like a good one. Typically, these conversations go like this:

Steve: *Hey, Andy, I've got a second interview coming up with WangoTech! They really seem to like me, and they pay well. I'm finally going to be making what I deserve.*

Andy: *Sounds cool, but I didn't think they had an office out here.*

Steve: *Well, it's down in the city, which is a good hour from Mayberry where I live. But I can listen to recorded books in the car, so that won't be so bad.*

Andy: *I guess not. But it's a programming job, right?*

Steve: *The ad says that it's for a "system administrator with programming skills," so I might not be doing programming right off. But I'll get some programming chops in, y'know?*

Andy: *I guess there's a chance. What kind of shop are they like? I know you love your BSD. Can you at least run a Mac and OS X?*

Steve: *(sigh) I don't think so. When they showed me around, it looked like all Windows everywhere. One of my first jobs would be to convert the intranet sites from Apache to Microsoft IIS. My boss-to-be said that the CTO back at corporate felt that open source was inherently unsafe. But I could probably have a little server as a skunkworks project.*

Andy: Back at corporate? How big are they? Your current shop is, what, a dozen programmers and two sysadmins?

Steve: Yeah, WangoTech is a big company. There's corporate and then three branch offices. The branch I'd be in has only 100 programmers. But that's the smallest branch, so we'd sort of have that startup feel!

Andy: So, what I'm hearing is that you're considering taking a job with three times the commute, doing sysadmin work instead of programming, and it's in a big, corporate, all-Windows, open source–unfriendly environment.

Steve: I guess it sounds bad, but I'll finally get paid what I deserve.

Andy: But I thought you liked it where you are now. Why aren't you paid what you deserve now?

Steve: My boss is just an idiot. He doesn't really respect me, and he doesn't think that my skills are up to snuff. My last review I got a 2 percent raise, and that's absurd. I've gotta get outta there.

Andy: It sounds like you don't want that job but rather a different job or, more precisely, a higher-paying job with more respect.

Steve: Yeah, I guess. But this one sounds OK, doesn't it?

Andy: I guess it could be, but I'm not you. I will point out that every downside I've mentioned has been countered with what seems to me to be a half-hearted explanation of how it won't be so bad. Were I in your situation, I wouldn't be so optimistic about that. You really think you could do well administering Windows and Exchange Server all day?

Steve: Well....

If you're not able to have this sort of inner dialogue with yourself, find someone who will be a good sounding board. It could be your spouse, a friend, a co-worker, or even your parents.[1] It should be someone who will honestly but compassionately listen to and challenge your plans, without giving you the answers.

---

1. I've found parents can be surprisingly wise. You may find they grow wiser the older you get.

You're looking for guidance, not someone who will tell you what to do.

This inner honesty is crucial to assessing your goals and wants. As technical problem solvers, we're accustomed to searching for the facts of a problem so that we can accurately solve and diagnose it. Without accurate facts, we solve the wrong problem or make the original problem even worse. Without being true to yourself, you do the same thing to your job search.

1.2 Be Honest with Others

Hiring books say it all the time, and I'll continue to beat the drum here: you must not lie or be false at any time. It is a sure recipe for getting fired or having a very unhappy relationship.

Don't fudge about what you can do, about what you know, or about what you've done in the past. Outright lies are easy to avoid, of course. It's the little fudging that's easier to try to get away with. Don't think you can say "yes" to "Do you know J2EE?" just because you've done Java and J2EE is Java. Don't think you can say "yes" because you can buy a copy of *J2EE for Dummies* on the way home and you think, how hard can it be to learn anyway? Don't think you can say "yes" because you read an online tutorial on J2EE and it looked pretty simple.

The problem with this type of factual lying, above any ethical issues, is that your lie *will* be caught. The follow-up question to "Do you know J2EE?" will probably be "Tell me about what J2EE projects you've done," and you're stuck for an answer. If it's not in the interview, some day on the job the boss will come to you with a J2EE problem, and you'll be exposed as a fraud. Both situations are far more uncomfortable and damaging than saying "no" up front.

> **Lying lays land mines that never go away.**

Sometimes candidates will try to get around unpleasant parts of their history. Maybe the résumé will say a position was from 2001–2003, when it was really only until 2002. Maybe when asked "Have you ever been fired?" a candidate will lie and say "no," hoping that the employer won't follow up. These deceptions are insidious because they follow the employee around forever. Say you've been on the job for a year, and one day out at lunch you mention to a co-worker that you got fired from a job a few years ago. That co-worker mentions it to the boss, who now knows that you've lied to him and either fires you immediately or never trusts you again.

My colleague Seth Gumble has a brutal story about a candidate who was dishonest in an interview and how poorly it turned out for everyone.

"I'll Try Hard!"
by Seth Gumble, IT director

I'd hired a programmer to migrate from PostgreSQL to Oracle on Solaris. I asked him in the interview "Do you know Oracle beyond Oracle Applications?" He said he did. "It looks like you've done most of your work on Windows. Do you know Unix?" Again, he said he did. "So, if I sit you down to start migrating our Postgres back end to an Oracle back end, all on Solaris, you can do that?" He said he could.

The first day, I show him his machine and give him his login. I tell him where the directory with the data files is, but he types it wrong. I tell him "You'll have to back up a directory." He doesn't know what I mean. I say, "Just type *see dee dot dot*," and he types out cd.. without the space, instead of cd ... We go around on this a few times, and I have to explain that there's a space after the cd. It turns out that he's never used a UNIX shell. He's only FTPed web pages to servers that happen to run UNIX.

I give him a day or two to try to catch on, but no luck. I call him into my office and explain, "Everyone is expecting me to move our site to an Oracle back end. You are making no progress. Do you think you'll ever get there?" He says, "I'll try hard!" I say, "I believe you, but I don't think you can try hard enough to get it done in three months given where you're at." He agreed that I made my expectations clear in the interview and that there was no way he was going to be able to do it. He was terminated after that meeting. I wound up having to do all the Oracle work myself because of the time lost hiring this guy.

Clearly, the candidate was dishonest, but in what way? Was he lying to himself, overestimating his abilities? Was he lying to Seth, knowing that he didn't have what it took but perhaps hoping that he would be able to learn on the fly, just by trying hard, if only he could get the job?

The lesson is clear: the truth will come out. It's better for all concerned to be honest up front.

There's one other way to be dishonest, and that's to pretend to be someone you're not. You must be yourself at all steps in the hiring process. If you live doing Extreme Programming, don't pretend that monolithic requirements documents make you happy. When you become the Real You once you start working, both you and your manager are going to be sorely disappointed.

1.3 Think Like the Boss

Put yourself in the shoes of your boss-to-be, the hiring manager, or the person who is going to be making the decision about your employment; this is the person for whom you'll likely be working for a long time. It makes sense to think exactly how she thinks. What does she want in an employee? How can you make her life easier? How can you make her look good? Your job is to make her look good.

"Make your boss look good" sounds crass, conniving, or political, but it's not. It's a mental shorthand for your higher-level goals. Your immediate job may be to write code, design web pages, or administer networks, but it's all in the service of making your department achieve its goals.

As a manager, my staff's job is to make me look good. My job is to make my boss, the senior director of IT, look good. His job is to make the VP of IT look good. His job is to make the president of the company look good. As each person meets the next level's goals, the organization's goals are furthered. It's the basis for any hierarchical organization. Whether there are two levels of hierarchy or ten in the organization, the principle is the same.

This makes it much easier to know how to deal with the company, and the hiring manager, when you're trying to get hired. You can focus with precision on what the hiring manager wants and how she wants it. Of course, you want to have some idea of what the company's needs are in the large, but you should focus on the hiring manager. You'll need to know when you prepare your company-specific résumé and prepare for the interview.

Understand the Hiring Process

In addition to understanding the boss's high-level goals in the company, you should understand the hiring process in general. Hiring someone is expensive and is not undertaken lightly. Labor costs are a significant part of the cost of running a business, and just getting the OK to hire is often a drawn-out process for the manager.

The manager will have a specific need that she needs to satisfy and will have to go to her boss with a proposal to add head count to the department. She'll have to show that the increased productivity of the department will offset the additional costs of salary, benefits, equipment, and space used. Often, a pain point will be the trigger for the hire. Perhaps she decides that the department needs a dedicated database administrator because programmers are spending too much time tending to the database to the detriment of programming schedules. Maybe unacceptable tech support call times prompt the addition of another support specialist. If you can find out what has prompted the hire (see Section 5.4, *Do Your Detective Work*, on page 94), you can tailor your end of the process to meet those needs.

Most hires won't be for new positions but will be replacing a previous employee who either left for a different job or was fired for not doing the job well enough. Finding out the background to these two scenarios will also help you frame and aim the process to your advantage.

Hiring someone is never arbitrary (at least in well-run companies). Understand the process, and use it to your advantage.

The Manager Wants to Hire You

Since you know that the manager has a problem to solve and has jumped through hoops to get to the point where she can start the hiring process and that the process is very time-consuming, it follows that *the hiring manager wants to hire you*. She might not want *you* specifically, but that's why the process is in place. She wants someone to be good enough to meet her needs so that she can get back to the real work of the department.

We all have better things to do than go through interviews.

As you go through the process, remember that the process for the manager is time-consuming and stressful, just as it is for you. Everything the hiring manager is doing is in the service of "I hope that this candidate is the one." Help her realize that you are.

Finally, read up on management and hiring as it applies to your industry. Johanna Rothman's *Hiring the Best Knowledge Workers, Techies, and Nerds* [Rot04] is a great overview of the hiring manager's side of desk. It pays to understand what your counterpart in the dance is thinking, and it may just give you some empathy for her while she puts you through the wringer.

1.4 Be a Problem Solver

Ken Blanchard's classic management book *The One Minute Manager* [BJ82] is an allegorical tale of business life. In one part, an employee comes to The Manager and says, "Sir, I have a problem," to which he replies, "Good, that's what you've been hired to solve." The employee came in looking for a solution to his problem, and the boss reminded him that problem solving is exactly why he is involved in the company at all.

Your boss-to-be is looking to hire you for one reason, and that's to solve problems for him. If all he needed was someone to do grunt work, to crank out some code, to string cable, or to dispense IP addresses, he could hire a trained monkey off the street to do it. What he really wants is someone to take care of those tasks *and* solve the problems that come up as part of them. He doesn't want someone who's going to say "Boss, there's a wall in the way of my cable running; what should I do?" but rather "I got the cabling completed, and I had a problem. Here's how I solved it."

My Printer Ran Out of Ink
by Andy Lester, your humble narrator

When I invite a candidate for a face-to-face interview, I always tell him to bring printed copies of sample code. I want it printed so that we can look at the code at my desk and discuss it. One morning, a candidate walked in at 9:10 for a 9 a.m. interview, thrust an orange 3.5" diskette at me, and without apology said,

"My printer ran out of ink this morning." Our interview was short and perfunctory before I showed him out.

Let's look at his sins. First, he was late, probably because he hadn't allowed enough time to get to the interview and for anything that might have come up, as I discuss in Section 7.6, *Prepare to Get to the Interview*, on page 135.

Second, in this short exchange he told me that he was not a problem solver. He told me he was unable to perform a simple assigned task and changed it to suit his own convenience. He told me that he didn't bother preparing for this part of the interview until that morning. He told me that he didn't have the foresight to have spare ink cartridges. He told me he didn't have the problem-solving savvy to stop at an Office Depot on the way to the interview.

Worst of all, he gave me his problem. He said, "I am unable to solve this problem, so I will give it to you. Here you go, Mr. Manager, print the code off this disk that your floppyless Macintosh can't read." Fortunately, I no longer had any interest in his code or hiring him at all.

You're probably acting like a problem solver already in your current job and day-to-day life, but you must *present yourself* as one to your future employer. Revisit your skills, and rethink how you look at what you can do. Your coding skills aren't as interesting as how you applied those coding skills to an especially difficult project. Your ability to maintain the network isn't as interesting as how you've created backup systems and contingency plans to head off future problems. Tracking project status is one thing, but getting those projects back on track in the face of crisis is quite another.

1.5 Sell Yourself

If you're like many programmers I've met, you probably sneered when you read that "Sell Yourself" heading. "Maybe for other people," you might have said," but I'm not going to sing and dance for someone just for a job. If they don't like me, that's fine; I'll go somewhere else."

Or maybe you think that selling yourself shows weakness or desperation. "If I go in there selling myself, they'll think I'm just a loser who has to talk about how cool I think I am."

That's not at all what selling yourself is about.

> **Selling yourself is something you do every day.**

Selling yourself doesn't mean to present something false or to try to get a job where you're not qualified. Indeed, doing so would violate two earlier rules, "Be honest with yourself" and "Be honest with others." It's about presenting the aspects of you and your capabilities that might otherwise be unknown to the person or company you're interested in working with. You're making sure that people know what you want them to know.

To a co-worker: *Let's go to lunch. There's a great Mexican place over on Route 120.*

To a friend: *Want to join our game night? We've got a good group, and I'm going to be DMing a cool new campaign I've been working on.*

To your daughter: *Sweetie, would you like to go to the zoo this weekend? They have a new dolphin exhibit.*

In each case, each spoken proposition could stand on its own ("Let's go to lunch."), but then evidence to support the proposition ("There's a great Mexican place...") is added. The speaker is selling the proposition, but there's nothing sleazy or desperate about it.

At work, and in the open source community, it's the same. Present a proposition and sell it.

To a project team: *I'll take care of the reporting subsystem. I've written one before, and I've been familiarizing myself with a few packages that we can use.*

To a mailing list: *I think that we should use the FooTest as the basis for the testing infrastructure. It scales to large test suites, and it's well maintained.*

To your boss: *The team lead position is a natural for me. Although I haven't been here the longest, I've developed a great rapport with the others, and you know that my estimation skills are spot on.*

When you're presenting a résumé, the proposition is "I think you should hire me," and the evidence is contained within your résumé, your cover letter, and your conversations with those who do the hiring. You're selling yourself.

Some people are not used to this idea. Geeks are often shy, and I've talked to many who have told me that it was hard to discuss their talents without feeling like they were bragging. Women can also run afoul of the perception, at least in the United States, that an assertive woman can be seen as "pushy" or "bitchy."

I understand these can be problems for some people. You still need to overcome them to be able to express your talents and history. If you aren't able to present your best aspects to a company, to a hiring manager, or to your circle of contacts, then you'll have fewer choices and opportunities than someone else who does. That person might even be less qualified than you are, but because your light is hidden under a bushel basket, nobody knows it.

The key is that selling yourself is an active pursuit. You're working actively to make known your assets and qualifications, and you're not relying on being asked for them. As well, you may be presenting qualifications that haven't been asked for but that would probably help the company.

1.6   Tell Stories and Give Samples of Your Work

The best way to sell yourself is to tell stories. Stories are evidence of who you are, what you can do, and how you've done it in the past. Samples of your work show that you're able to deliver the goods. Most important, stories and samples let the person hearing the story make the assessment about you.

When faced with the daunting task of summarizing themselves, whether on paper in a résumé or face-to-face in an interview, job hunters often fall into the trap of trying to encapsulate everything into a few simple, pithy phrases.

I've seen these meaningless chestnuts far too often:

- "I'm a hard worker."

- "I have a strong work ethic."

- "I'm reliable."

- "I'm a good listener."

- "I work well with others."

- "I take pride in my work."

The hiring manager's mental response, assuming his eyes haven't glazed over, is likely to be "You and everyone else, pal." Is there anyone out there who would not feel justified in using all of these assessments to describe themselves?

Descriptions that can apply to anyone are worthless.

The next response to such vague summarizations is "According to whom?" A "hard worker" at a big faceless corporation or a government 9-to-5 job may be very different from a "hard worker" at a startup or at a video game company.

Instead of simply assessing yourself as a "hard worker," give evidence and let the interviewer make up her own mind. Include points that make clear you were a hard worker, without you having to say "I worked hard." For example: "I recently completed a five-month, 50,000-line conversion project. Even though we lost one of the four team members with only three weeks left, we pulled together to make the deadline." Big project, hard work, no self-assessment, just the facts, ma'am.

Strong work ethic? Explain it: "A few weeks ago, my team rolled out an upgrade to Office in our 300-seat location. We did it over the weekend to minimize work disruption. Sunday night we had to order in some pizzas, but Monday morning everyone was able to come in and get work at 8 a.m. sharp."

Every manager wants reliable employees: "My projects are consistently done on time, never more than 10 percent over budget. Here are the planned vs. actual charts for the last three projects I worked on." Then you can show the actual work products from your portfolio.[2]

Working well with others is a hoary cliché, but it's critical in almost any job: "As a web page designer, I usually work with

---

2. See Section 7.4, *Prepare a Relevant Portfolio*, on page 125.

three or four different teams throughout the week. They're all very different in their makeup, but I work hard at fitting in with each as necessary. Ted in marketing even sent me a gracious thank-you note for my work, which I was very proud of." The note itself would be good to have in the back of your portfolio.

When it comes to the pride you take in your work, you need not explain at all. Your résumé and interview should be enough. The pride you take in yourself and your accomplishments must shine through without additional words being necessary.

Use recent examples when possible over stories from years past. Emphasize teamwork and other people, which every manager should have high on her list of important attributes. Document facts that let the interviewer draw her own conclusion about you and your value to her company. Her own opinion that you're a "hard worker" is far more valuable than your own proclamation of it.

The previous examples were taken from an interview setting, but they apply to any printed work as well. On a résumé, you'll have less room to stretch out verbally, but you can certainly replace your "Reliable worker" bullet point with "Completed 90 percent of projects on time and never more than 10 percent over estimates."

We'll look at more specifics in Chapter 3, *Résumé Content: Getting the Words Down*, on page 35 and in Chapter 8, *The Interview*, on page 139.

1.7 Be Positive

Every job book says to never badmouth a previous employer. Hearing a candidate griping about the place they just left leaves an interviewer wondering what she'll be like once she's joined the team.

That's good advice, but it's not enough. You must be unfailingly positive in all your dealings.

Nobody likes a complainer, except for people who are no fun to work with anyway. People who complain are like Debbie Downer from *Saturday Night Live*, who always has something negative to say, no matter the topic.

Her morose whining was played for laughs, but it was funny only because we've all heard people like this too often:

J. Random Hacker at lunch with his buddies: *I can't believe how dumb the marketing department is. They're still trying to run Windows Vista on three-year-old Pentium IIIs. Not that we have it much better since we're stuck with....*

What you may see as just commiserating with your buddies, or "blowing off steam," is likely demoralizing to others and certainly does nothing to build up your own morale. It might feel good in the short term, but over time it's a definite negative both to you and your team. People will remember your negative attitude over the long term, including your manager. A good manager will do whatever she can to keep toxic attitudes out of the workplace, and that includes you and your griping.

> Whiners tell the world, "I don't control my life."

Whiners also come across as people with an external focus of control, acted upon by the world, rather than acting upon the world themselves. Blamers are the people who see problems as not theirs to deal with and put the problem on others. The last thing you want to be seen as is a complainer.

The best way to start being positive is to not discuss problems that have no direct bearing on you or that you cannot fix. There's no point in worrying about the problems of others.

When discussing problems that do relate to you, then discuss what you've done to fix them or how you've gotten work done in the face of the problem. Problems you've faced in the past will come up in an interview, and you need to explain how you've worked to solve them, even if you were unsuccessful.

Interviewer: *It sounds like your department had problems with losing track of bugs. That must have been frustrating.*

You: *It was. We even had the head of accounting come over and chew out our team leader because we lost track of a showstopper. I had tried for weeks to get my boss to let us set up an instance of Bugzilla, but he said we couldn't even think about it until the end of the project. So, I got together with the guy in the next cube and tracked bugs via text files in a Subversion project. It was low-tech, but it saved us some real time.*

Note how here even though your boss has frustrated you, you've explained the solution you made happen in spite of it. You haven't said "Boy, my boss made a bad decision," even though you may have said or thought it at the time.

More important than maximizing your employment options, following the "Be positive" rule will probably make you a happier person over time.

1.8 Moving Ahead

I'll refer to these rules throughout the book, but none is more important than "Be honest with yourself." Keep it in mind as you start the next chapter.

Chapter 2

What Do You Want in a Job?

I was ready to leave my job. I had reached a plateau in my professional development at my company. My boss clearly had no interest in using any more of my skills. I reported to the department head, and it seemed likely that he was going to install a new supervisor over me. The writing was on the wall, so I started looking.

My job was doing web applications in ColdFusion under Windows, and I was itching to work with Perl in Unix or Linux. One Sunday as I scanned the *Chicago Tribune*'s listings, I saw a job that spoke to me.

> Perl programmer wanted with web application experience. We use mod_perl under Solaris.

It sounded perfect! I contacted the recruiter offering the job, and he brought me down to his office to meet with him the next morning. The recruiter thought I was a good candidate and sent me to the far outreaches of Chicago to meet with the hiring manager at 1 p.m. We hit it off, and by 4:30 p.m., before I'd even reached home, I had a job offer for 20 percent more than I was making. I was ecstatic and accepted immediately. A few weeks later, I started at my new position.

Fast-forward two months. I was miserable. One morning I called my wife, and as we talked about my dissatisfaction, I realized that my situation was such that it couldn't possibly get better. I walked into my boss's office and said, "I'm sorry, but I have to leave." He tried to get me to stay, but I knew it couldn't work. Ten minutes later I'd packed up my stuff and was out the door.

That decision cost me. I had no other job lined up, and I'd over-estimated the ease with which I could get hired. Worst of all, it was early December. Businesses all but shut down in December when it comes to hiring as managers and decision makers go on holiday vacations. I was glad to be out of that situation, but it cost me a few months of salary.

What went wrong? I ask audiences for their ideas when telling this story at conferences. I'd had a great programming job doing what I wanted, and I was making great money at it. What could have been so terrible? Why was my situation so grim? What made me up and quit? And how had I not realized that it would be so bad? Audience members offer a wide range of suggestions:

- "Your boss was an idiot."
- "It was all death march projects."
- "You weren't working on any projects at all."
- "The company was poorly managed."
- "It was maintenance programming only."[1]
- "The hours were awful. You worked lots of overtime."
- "It was a terrible location, and the commute was brutal."
- "The company was insolvent and was going to go under soon."
- "You weren't allowed to work with open source."
- "Your co-workers were jerks and idiots."
- "You weren't actually qualified for the job."
- "You didn't get to use any creativity."
- "They had unreasonable expectations of you."

None of these was the problem. Although the commute was rough, I could live with that if I was otherwise happy with the job. No, the problem was that I wasn't interested in what the company was doing, and I wasn't part of a team.

I'd accepted a job working for a financial services firm. There were a dozen investors watching quote boards and CNN all day, figuring out how to play the markets. The aura was one of extreme competitiveness. Aggressive macho posturing permeated everything. Worse, there was no sense of teamwork. I

---

1. I say that all programming is maintenance programming, but that's a topic for another book.

worked on solo projects, and half the team would only talk to people of their own nationality.

More important, I didn't have any interest in the industry. I'd left a company that wrote software for children's libraries, which I found very fulfilling, and gone to one that made money for rich people.

I have nothing against making money, and I'm glad that my 401(k) fund is managed by people who love it, but I know (now) that it's not the industry or environment for me.

The lesson here is "Don't take a job that doesn't give you what you want." The underlying corollary is "You can't get what you want 'til you know what you want." But how do you know what you want, what's important, what matters? That's the focus of this chapter.

But before we go on, let's have a little crash course in human motivational theory.

2.1 A Crash Course in Work Motivation Theory

In 1943, psychologist Abraham Maslow popularized the concept of a hierarchy of psychological needs for humans. He proposed that humans have basic needs that motivate them, grouped into six categories. From highest and most advanced, to lowest and most basic, they are as follows:

- Self-actualization
- Cognitive
- Ego/esteem
- Social
- Safety
- Physiological

Maslow discussed these in general terms of the natural world, but they apply to your working life as well. For example, the "Safety" need may not refer to physical safety at a desk job, but job security certainly may. For more on his hierarchy, the Wikipedia article[2] is a fine introduction.

---

2. http://en.wikipedia.org/wiki/Maslow%27s_hierarchy_of_needs

Similar to Maslow's hierarchy, Frederick Herzberg's Motivation-Hygiene Theory[3] looks to explain what motivates workers. He found that some some aspects of a job are motivators; that is, they encourage workers to do more. Other aspects are hygiene factors, such that their absence will result in dissatisfaction, but their presence is not a motivator. For example, getting paid and having reliable equipment are hygiene factors, not motivators. Interesting work and being able to learn new technology are usually motivators.

Although Maslow and Herzberg's theories are similar, Herzberg's categories are not a simple superset of Maslow's. Although "basic needs" roughly equates to "hygiene factors," and "growth needs" equates to "motivators," there is overlap. For example, Herzberg would say that esteem from colleagues is a motivator, but Maslow calls esteem from others a basic need.

As you consider what is important to you in a job, consider each aspect of a job and where it fits in Maslow's hierarchy and whether it's a hygiene factor or motivator *for you*. I find that these two categorizations help me see working life more clearly.

2.2 Dig In to What You're Looking For

Now that we have a foundation to understand your motivations, let's look at possible factors that go into your vision of what a job should be. I'm going to list a dozen or so motivators and conditions that may or may not enter into your decision-making process about the job hunt. This list is only partial, because I can't possibly know your situation, or anyone else's. The list shows some of the more common ones, but they're starting points. You have to examine your own situation, your own life, and your own ideals.

> "Should" puts others in control of your life.

As you examine your life, your job, and your job hunt, be wary of the word *should* cropping up in your thoughts. It's an insidious word that can steer you wrong, using your understanding of how others perceive you to drive your life. Take the simple sentence "I should learn

---

3. http://en.wikipedia.org/wiki/Motivator-Hygiene_theory

Java." Replace the word *should* with something more specific, more descriptive. Is your "should" a positive one?

- "I would like to learn Java."
- "My career options get broader if I learn Java."
- "I can make more money if I learn Java."

Or is it a negative "should," based on what you think others think and imagined norms?

- "I've been programming for ten years; I should know Java."
- "I think that most other people know Java, so I should, too."
- "I'm embarrassed that I don't know Java."

You can replace "knowing Java" with "making $100,000/year" or "being in management," but the results are the same: living by "should" lets your life be controlled by others. The negative, imagined "shoulds" allow the expectations, real or imagined, of other people dictate your life.

As you read through this list, be completely honest about your motivations and your concerns. Your future job is a relationship far too important to let it be tainted by self-delusion. It's no different from assessing what's important to you in a romantic relationship. Maybe you're only attracted to tall blondes or you don't like being around people who drink or you want your mate to share your religious beliefs. You may think "That's shallow thinking" or "That shouldn't matter if everything else about my mate is good," but countless marriages have wound up in divorce because of exactly that sort of wishful thinking. In the same way, it's foolish to think that your loathing of Windows, your need to be a big fish in a small pond, or specific salary requirements can be ignored in the long run.

Consider also that not all your motivations have to be satisfied by your day job. Perhaps you can scratch some of your itches outside of work. In my off hours (and some of my on hours), I've worked for the Perl Foundation doing public relations work, as well as many more hours working on various open source projects, and I find that this serves my internal needs.

My Extra-curricular Activities

by Ricardo Signes, programmer, Bethlehem, Pennsylvania

Not only do I use extra-curricular activities to do some of the work-like things that I want to do, but I sometimes think that's a better plan. I want to play with different programming languages or language libraries from time to time, but work is not always the place for that. I futz around with Haskell, Scheme, or Erlang in my off time to make sure that work is always a place with consistent standards (thus scratching the "work should be sane" itch!).

I also like to teach other people how to do what I do, but my company is small and doesn't have any real junior programmers. I make do by speaking at conferences and user groups. I get to teach a lot more people that way, and I get free admission or a free beer!

Finally, none of these needs stand alone. Each is related to something else, in a web of interconnected motivators.

2.3 The Motivation Worksheet

Take some time to make a worksheet that's a brain dump of your motivations. This worksheet will act as a guide for you as you search for jobs and a sort of compass for keeping you on track as you evaluate opportunities. It will be a snapshot of what matters to you in those times that you might otherwise forget.

As you go through the process, think about your needs without looking at them under the harsh light of "reality," where you're likely to say, "What are the chances of my actually getting a job as a game designer for Linux making $100,000/year?" You're looking only at your motivations, not finding a job out of them. You especially want to go through this worksheet exercise *before* you are looking at a specific job, if possible. Your self-reflection may wind up filtered by a situation at hand.

Your worksheet need not be complicated. It can be a simple list of factors and some sort of indicator of relative importance. There's no wrong way to do this, so long as it's honest and fits your needs.

Here's what a worksheet for me would look like today in 2009 and twelve years earlier in 1997. I've listed many factors and assigned a relative importance from 1–10 for each. A 10 is effectively mandatory, and a 1 is almost inconsequential. Of course, you can add or remove whatever factors you want. It's your worksheet.

Andy's Needs	2009	1997
Salary	7	9
Good health benefits	10	3
Location	6	2
Strong team, co-workers	10	4
Contributing to open source software	6	2
Using non-Windows technology	9	0
Autonomy	7	10
...	...	

Note how as my life and career change, the importance of certain factors change as well. Ten years ago, I didn't care about good health benefits, but I didn't have a child, either. Money was more important then than now, because I used it as a sort of benchmark to see how I was doing in life. I've learned a bit more since then.

2.4 What Motivates You? A Dozen Factors to Consider

Here's a list of factors that most people find important to consider as they search for a job. I urge you to have pen and paper at hand as you read and jot down what matters to you and a relative importance for each item. In addition to the factor's importance, note the specifics of what is necessary for you.

Money

Money is perhaps the most obvious motivator, but it's not always a matter of how much you can get. Money also comes in many different forms.

You need to know what your financial requirements are, and that means you must know what minimum base salary you need. Sometimes people say "Salary isn't important, as long as the work is interesting," but that's just not true. Maybe you don't have to make $200,000/year, but you wouldn't work for

$5/hour as long as the work was interesting, would you? You need to know what your bottom-line minimum is.

Money may not just be salary. Some companies may pay a yearly bonus, which may or may not be based on performance of either you or the company. Some may pay a signing bonus. All these factor into your total monetary compensation. Add a 401(k), discussed below, and you have many variables to juggle.

What to know: what minimum salary you require and what range you expect to make.

Benefits

Other forms of compensation figure into your financial needs. Maybe you have a family with specific health-care needs, so the type of health insurance offered makes a difference. To a healthy, single 25-year-old, this may be nearly irrelevant, compared to a 40-year-old with a 6-year-old daughter. The differences between HMO, PPO, and other group health insurance plans may make a big difference in your long-term happiness with a company.

Retirement plans like 401(k) and 403(b) that a company pays into are effectively free money. A job paying $50,000 that lets you max out your 401(k) at 10 percent that matches dollar for dollar is actually paying you $55,000. You're receiving only $45,000 since $5,000 comes out of your paycheck, but $10,000 is going into your 401(k) account.

Stock and stock options are deferred compensation that relate to how well the company is doing. You may be offered perks like health club memberships, company cars, discounts on products the company sells, and so on. The number of ways that you can be paid are endless.

What to know: benefits you must have, including any specifics about types of health coverage you must have; amount of 401(k) participation you want to take advantage of; and any benefits important to you.

Location

Your workplace's location is relevant in both a macro and micro sense. In the macro sense, if you're in Iowa and plan on staying there, you're not going to be searching for jobs in California (or at least jobs that require you to move to California). Your macrogeographic requirements may be based on family, climate, or any of a number of different factors.

In most cases, you'll probably be looking for a job in the same general geographic area, but there are considerations there as well. Maybe you don't want to have a commute longer than thirty minutes or to have to fight city traffic. Maybe a job in the hustle and bustle of a major city is something you can't bear to imagine. Before you say "an hour in the car isn't so bad," consider that hour every morning and then every night on the way home after a hard day. For rail commuters, ask your commuting friends how many actually use the train time to "catch up on some reading."

What to know: how far you are willing to commute every day, in terms of both distance and time, and in what form of transportation.

Pride and Prestige

For some, the allure of having a Google business card or being able to say "I work for Apple" can be intoxicating. If you're one of those people, make sure you look at the situation with open eyes. Maybe you have sights set on Google, but once you look at it, Yahoo! is just as cool. The work itself may be the source of your pride. It may not matter if you're working at Apple if you, or your friends, see your work as boring old sysadmin work.

If you think this sounds egotistical, stop and make sure that it doesn't apply to you. Recognition from one's peers is a powerful motivation, and there's nothing wrong with it. Be honest with yourself in your assessment of what drives you.

Maybe it doesn't matter what the work is if you can't tell anyone. I have a friend who worked at a major hardware company who was telling me of work **Know your internal motivators.** she was proud of but she couldn't show me, because restrictions prohibited her from showing anyone outside of the company.

What to know: your internal motivators.

Important Work

After my two-month stint at the financial services company, I realized how important it was that my work was fulfilling to me. I felt good in what I was doing, helping school libraries, in a way that wasn't there in a financial company. My friend Tom Limoncelli took a pay cut to work for a presidential candidate he believed in (see Section 10.2, *Politics*, on page 188). Your motivators may be different.

At the other end, perhaps you don't have any real motivators in who you would want to work for, but there are certain companies you would not work for, such as a military contractor, a tobacco company, or a seller of pornography. Although these may not be worth noting on your initial self-assessment of what you want, if you come across a company that raises this sort of flag in your mind, examine it carefully.

The type of work may make a difference as well. Perhaps you want to work on projects only for products or services that the company sells. Maybe you don't want to work on accounting applications because that's only back-room programming that isn't very important, or maybe you see accounting applications as a way to use your skills at envisioning information to help management increase profitability.

What to know: what "important" work looks like to you.

Type of Work to Be Done

The type of work may be different from what work is important. Programmers are often motivated by sexy products and projects. Maybe you're the kind of programmer who hates working on back-end program internals, and you want to work only on sexy interfaces. Conversely, you could be like me, thriving on building infrastructure and tools on which others can hang their sexy interfaces.

Either way, it's something you'll want to know about by the time you leave the interview, if not before.

What to know: the kinds of projects that excite you and make you want to come to work each day.

Company Size/Department Size

Size of the company usually has a big effect on how things are done. Bigger companies tend to be more rule-bound. Smaller companies usually give employees more autonomy. Bigger companies may have more room for advancement, but it may be a more political process than in smaller ones. Bigger companies typically have onerous IT departments that lock down everything related to computer hardware and software. Smaller companies may not care what you run on your desktop.

On the personal level, you may be the type of person who wants to be a big fish in a small pond. You love it when people say, "I don't know; go ask Susan about that, she's the expert." Conversely, you may prefer to go through your day just getting your work done and not standing out.

What to know: how big a company, a department, or a team that you want to work for.

Your Co-Workers

Do you need a well-oiled, high-performing team to make your life complete? Or can you get by with co-workers who fly below your soaring heights? How important is it to have co-workers who are more talented than you to challenge your skills? Do you get along with everyone? Or will one jerk on the team ruin your whole day?

The importance of social interactions at work can't be ignored. You may think this: "I have a job to get work done, not have a social club." Although that may be true, Maslow still puts it as one of the four basic human needs, not one of the two higher-order growth needs. You'll be with your co-workers for forty hours a week or more, which may well be more waking hours than you spend with your spouse. Don't discount this one. On the other hand, bad people come and go through good companies.

Technical challenges from one's co-workers can also be an important part of job satisfaction. I've talked with many dissatisfied people who complain with this: "I hate being the smartest person in the place."

What to know: who you want to work with and who you want to avoid.

Technology Used

Nothing affects a techie's day-to-day work life more than the tools she has to use. Unless you're ambivalent and are just as happy working in Windows with Visual Studio as you are running Emacs under Solaris, dig into this in your interview. (See Section 7.5, *Prepare Your Questions to Ask*, on page 130.) However, don't expect that the company will match your desires exactly. Maybe they use ksh instead of bash, or maybe they're running on Macintoshes instead of Windows (if you're lucky!). Any new job is going to take some adjusting to, and tech differences are part of that.

In fact, you may specifically look for differences as a motivator for the job. Maybe you've used only Linux in the past and the chance to work in a BSD environment would be a great addition to your résumé.

Sometimes the technology may be very limiting. Perhaps all machines in the company run only a very specific version of Windows, and free software is unheard of. Conversely, but also limiting, employees of the Free Software Foundation only use software that matches certain stringent licensing requirements.

What to know: what systems, languages, and other tools you enjoy using. What you want to learn going forward.

Autonomy and Direction

Techies tend to crave independence and autonomy more than most, sometimes to the degree where there can be grave misunderstandings between the employee and management. Some programmers consider a daily check-in from a project manager to say, "Hey, how's the project going?" to be "micromanagement." On the flip side, I've worked where management was so hands-off that management let the programmers do whatever they wanted and hoped that something good came out of it.

What to know: imagine what a good relationship with management means to you.

Dress Code

This is much the same as autonomy, but it's such a common concern among tech folks that it deserves a note of its own. The war with management over dress codes has been around since the first programmers came to work in torn jeans and a flannel shirt. Techs tend to hate ties and prefer to dress casually. The business world has drifted away from the button-down dress codes of decades past, and not just for programmers.

How comfortable do you have to be? Do you bridle at the thought of management telling you what you can and can't wear? Any job at all, unless you work out of your house, is going to have a dress code of some kind, even if unwritten. Is it that important to be able to wear your Slayer 1997 tour T-shirt to work? If so, you limit your options, but make sure you know that about yourself.

What to know: your sartorial minimums. Whether you can get by wearing a tie every day. What about Dockers? Pantyhose?

Working Hours

Day in, day out, you're going to have a schedule of some form. How much does the company's schedule mesh with when you want to work?

Rigidity of the working schedule may make a difference. Can you work Monday through Friday from 7:45 to 4:15? How about whenever you want, so long as the work is done? Chances are you'll get something that's somewhere in the middle, although sysadmins and help desk staff with outward-facing responsibilities often have less flexibility.

Are you able to do weekend and after-hours work? What is "after-hours?" How much are people expected to work if not a rigid set of office hours? Are you seen as a slacker for working fewer than ten hours each day? What about being on call? Will you have to be available for crisis handling, even on a rotating basis?

Flexibility with family can be critical. Can you take some hours in the afternoon to go to your kid's doctor appointment, or does it require paperwork and invocation of the Family and Medical

Leave Act? What the job ad calls "family-friendly" may not meet your expectations.

What to know: you and your family's requirements for how much time you can spend at the office and how flexible you need your company to be in relation to working hours.

And Many, Many More

The previous dozen issues are just to get you thinking about commonly considered aspects of employment. This list is hardly inclusive. Here are some others that may trigger ideas for your worksheet:

- Fun factor: Is the work fun or a drudge?

- Career advancement: Do you have a path to advance in the company? Or does that not concern you?

- Responsibility and/or power of the position: Is it important for you to lead, or are you happy creating the work?

- Personal growth/training/education: Where do you want to grow personally? Will the company support that?

- Company stability: Is the company likely to be around in the long term? What's your tolerance for risk?

- Industry stability: Is the industry stable or subject to fluctuations in the economy?

- Stepping stone to future jobs: Do you need a certain kind of job to reach future goals?

You'll come up with more as you work on your sheet. You'll come up with even more as you search for a job. You'll find yet more as you interview for a job. It's a never-ending project, and you should treat it as such. Add and remove factors from your list, and change rankings as your discover more about yourself. People change, perceptions change, and certainly the job market changes.

Understanding what you want is an iterative process, just like writing software. You'll create a first version, use it, see what you don't like modify, and repeat.

2.5 Now Go Beta Test Your Worksheet

Your alpha test for your worksheet is to run it past a spouse or close friend. Now comes the real test: searching for a job. Although you won't necessarily use the sheet of paper as a checklist while job hunting, going through the steps of creating that physical object will likely have helped clarify the most important aspects in your mind. Now you're ready to start looking.

Chapter 3

Résumé Content: Getting the Words Down

Conventional wisdom says it's deceptively simple to write your résumé: figure out your objective, list your college degree, jot down the jobs you've had, put some bullet points with "action words" under each job, and slap "references available upon request" at the bottom. If inspiration isn't coming to you, you can model it on one from a book with a title like *1,001 Résumés for All Occasions*. Voilà! You have your résumé!

Wrong, wrong, wrong!

Your résumé is far too crucial to your job search to leave to such a slapdash approach. Remember that you're selling yourself. Your résumé is your most important selling tool. It's there in your place, telling your potential employer about who and what you are, when you're not able to do it yourself. More people will see your résumé during the hiring process than will meet you.

Your résumé has to work on two different levels. First, it must be clear enough for the hiring manager, or whoever screens the résumés for him, to find the good stuff in it and to decide to put you in the "Maybe" pile. When I go through résumés, they're in my email inbox, and as I go through them, I make an initial cut: it's worth printing to paper, or it's not. Anything that isn't immediately obvious to me as being at least a viable candidate for a job is deleted and never looked at again.

After the initial yes/no filtering process, your résumé and cover letter will be referred to often throughout the rest of the hiring process. The hiring manager will take notes on it and will pass copies around to others involved in the process. Depending on the hiring process of the company, it may get passed all the way up the chain of command to the company president for final approval. Your résumé may be scrutinized by dozens of people, many of them perfectly happy to notice and point out its flaws.

3.1 Before You Write Your Résumé...

Before we think about the parts of your résumé, remember this: you're probably going to need it in three formats: Word for most companies of any size, plain text, and HTML for your website.

I know it may make you cringe to have repeated data. Most techies are interested in doing things as efficiently, and with as little rework, as possible.[1] You're not alone; it hurts me to have to have multiple copies in multiple formats, too, but it's the way it is. I know that Word, especially, is an odious format, but unless you're dealing only with a very few companies and they're especially anti-Microsoft, you're likely to be asked for a Word document. So, in this chapter we'll focus on writing the textual part of your résumé before worrying about specifics of visual presentation.

We're still going to cover presentation, because presentation *is* content, especially for a job as detail-oriented as a technical job, but not until we're sure what you want to say. For now, just think of your résumé as plain text, with abstract organization like "sections" and "headings" and "bullets."

For now, just think text.

Prepare to Write More Than One Résumé

You're also not writing your résumé, singular. You're writing the base from which you'll create specialized résumés for each job you apply for.

---

1. Larry Wall, the creator of Perl, says the three virtues of a programmer are laziness, impatience, and hubris. Minimizing rework is the best kind of laziness.

If you're applying to more than one job, you need to have more than one résumé. Different jobs and different companies all have different requirements. Even if you're applying for two jobs both called "applications programmer" at the same company, they're not the same job.

I often get asked for résumé help, and it's always a vague request: "How does my résumé look? Is this good? Should I change anything?" My answer is always the same: "What's the job you're applying for?"

A résumé must speak to its specific audience, tailored both for the company you're applying to and for the specific job you're looking to do. Say you're looking for a job as a Unix system administrator. The résumé you send with your cover letter may be tailored differently if you're applying to a small startup than if you're applying to the corporate headquarters of a large insurance company or the information services department of your local community college.

The details of the position will also dictate how your résumé looks. If the job ad states that you need to have a Microsoft Certified IT Professional (MCITP) certification, then you'd better put the details of your MCITP near the top of the résumé. If you were applying for a Unix sysadmin position, your MCITP would be noted in a section of "training and accomplishments." And if you were trying to work for an organization like the Free Software Foundation, you might even leave the MCITP off your résumé entirely.

For now, keep notes on everything that could go on a résumé for you, even if it's not directly related to a position you have your eye on right now. Keep a notes file that you can refer to so that you can swap in and out relevant data when the time comes.

Don't Fear the Résumé Police

Job hunters seem to think that the Résumé Police are out there. Truncheons in hand, magically seeing every résumé written, these officers of conformity seek out and punish those who do not follow the Golden Format when writing a résumé. At least, that's what it seems like when people ask "What order do my jobs have to go in" or "Is it OK if I make it longer than two pages" or "Do I need to have an 'Education' section?"

> **There's no one "right" way to write a résumé.**

I promise, the Résumé Police do not exist. Your ninth-grade English teacher, who made sure that your research paper had a bibliography that exactly matched a certain style, will not be scrutinizing your résumé.

There's no law that says you must have certain sections, in a certain order, or that you have to list the months as well as the years when listing positions. Although there are certain conventions followed and certain sorts of information that people will expect to be able to find on your résumé, you need not fear the swift wrath of Mrs. Cruella and her Red Pen of Correction.

Question everything about your résumé and how it's constructed, even what you find in résumé books, even this book. Let your own judgment be the ultimate guide.

3.2 Writing a Résumé Is Not Speedy

This is a long process. You're not going to write a good résumé in one sitting. You're not going to assemble a good portfolio of your work, which I'll discuss in Section 7.4, *Prepare a Relevant Portfolio*, on page 125, all at once. You're not going to make a list of what you're looking for in a job in one sitting. They may take days, with an initial burst of activity, and a week or two of updates as you think more about it.

Start writing your résumé immediately, if you don't have one already, but come back to it frequently. Keep a scraps file of items you'd like to add to the résumé or that you've removed as irrelevant. Tend to your base résumé like a garden, planting new items and removing old items, as you think of them.

Take notes of what you see around you in your job search. Are certain buzzwords more popular in ads? Perhaps those are the aspects of your résumé to play up. Evaluate the reaction to your résumé after each interview. Don't let your résumé fall into disrepair and irrelevance.

3.3 The Sections of Your Résumé

Even though there's no one right way to do a résumé, the résumé reader will expect there to be certain information about you. Therefore, your résumé should contain, at minimum, the following sections:

- Contact block
- Professional summary
- Work experience
- Education
- Other achievements outside of work (optional, if your work experience is thin)
- List of buzzwords and skills

These are the areas that employers are looking for and find to be most important. The order of sections in your résumé should be determined by their relative importance. Put more important sections toward the top of the résumé, where they'll be more likely to be seen.

The most important text in your résumé is your contact information, so that is always first. Without a way to contact you, there's no reason to have a résumé.

After that, you'll have a professional summary that lets the reader see you in a nutshell. Beyond those two, the order depends on your background and the job for which you're applying.

Let's look at each of these sections in depth.

The Contact Block

The contact block usually doesn't get much thought, but it's the most important part of the résumé. If the company can't contact you, you can't get hired.

At the very least, the top of your résumé needs to have your name, email address, phone number, and street address. If you want to list two phone numbers, one land and one cell, that's OK. Don't bother with more than that, and certainly don't include a fax number.

What Name Should I Use?

Think about what name you use on your résumé if you have more than one. My given name is Andrew Lester, but I'm Andy to everyone except the government, so Andy is the name I use on my résumé. More important, Andy is the name that you'll find me under when searching the web for what I've blogged, code I've written, and so on.

If you have a married name or a hyphenated name, put on the résumé the one that gives the hiring manager the best chance of finding good information about you on the Internet. If your legal name is Margaret Smith-Widget but on LinkedIn and elsewhere you go by Peggy Widget, then searches by interested employers are going to come up empty.

Absolutely do not list your current work number as a contact number. Set up voicemail on your home number if you must, but you don't want to be taking job-hunting calls at work.

The Professional Summary

An "elevator pitch" is a high-level overview of something such that you could explain it to someone during a ride in an elevator. The pitch encapsulates something you want to sell into a brief explanation. It could be a product, a project, your company, or, in this case, you as a job candidate. The key to the elevator pitch is that the recipient's time is short and very valuable, and brevity is a must if you're to fit in the most important aspects of your proposal. Details can come later, once the prospect is interested.

Imagine you get on the elevator, and there's a hiring manager who recognizes you as a candidate because you have a big name tag that says Bob Smith. "You're interested for working for us, Smith? Tell me about yourself, but make it quick! I'm busy, and we'll be at my floor in twenty seconds."

Get a Decent Email Address

Any email correspondence to a prospective employer should be from your personal email address. Don't even think of sending mail from your current job's email address. Your current employer may well be monitoring email, but worse, few things are tackier than getting email from bob.smith@bobscurrentcompany.com. If you don't have your own email address, go to Google's Gmail* and sign up for a free account.

Before sending mail, consider that your email address is part of the presentation of who you are to your future employer. If your current email address is mr_beer_bong@gmail.com, get a second one for business correspondence.

---

*. http://gmail.com

You give him your elevator pitch. You tell him, "I have twelve years of software development experience, eight of them in your industry. I've led teams before, from three to eight members. I'm an expert in Perl and have written seven modules for the CPAN. And, I've had a couple of articles published in magazines like *Dr. Dobbs* and *The Perl Journal*." DING! The elevator car stops, and the hiring manager steps toward the opening doors. "Sounds good, Smith, I'll look into you more closely." Turn this scenario into printed words on a résumé, and you have your professional summary at the top of your résumé.

You may get only twenty seconds of skim time to make an impression on the person reading your résumé before she moves on to the next one. Whether it's the hiring manager herself or someone in human resources filtering out submissions, time is critical.

Someone looking at your résumé needs a reason to read the whole thing. Anyone advertising for a job is inundated with résumés. Imagine a hiring manager who's put an ad in the Sunday *Chicago Tribune* or placed an ad on

> No one will read your résumé word for word unless he's given a reason to do so.

Monster. Overnight, he may have an email inbox with 100 to 200 résumés. Now he has to weed through all the junk that has been sent to find the good stuff. That junk can include entirely unqualified candidates, sales reps from offshore out-sourcers looking for business, people who are geographically too far away, and so on.

You may be a unique and beautiful snowflake, but the hiring manager is swamped with a blizzard of snowflakes that all look the same to him. Your job is to catch his eye. That's why a fluff-free summary of who you are, and what specific value you will bring to the reader, should be the first thing he sees on your résumé.

Note how everything you said in your elevator pitch was a demonstrable and quantifiable achievement and entirely free of fluff. At no point would you say, "I'm a hard worker, sir!" because he'd growl back "Yeah, you and everyone else, Smith!" (See Appendix A, on page 235, for more to avoid.) You also didn't list every language that you'd ever read an article on or every operating system you'd ever typed a command into.

For a quick way to write your summary, start with three or four bullet points:

- Summary of experience
- Two or three different points of expertise
- College degrees and/or certifications, if they significantly add to your appeal

Summary of Experience

Probably the most important item to get out in front of the hiring manager is your level of experience, expressed in years of work, or months if fewer than two years. The hiring manager has a good idea of what she's looking for in a candidate, and years of experience is probably at the top of that definition.

The experience bullet will tell how long you've been working in the field, with specifics of industry or type of work if possible. Here are some examples:

- Three years of Solaris system administration for a Fortune 500 company

- Seven years software development in C/C++ writing library automation software
- Five years of user interface design

The specific wording of these bullets may change depending on the target of your résumé. You want to emphasize certain parts of your background as they relate to the job you're applying for. For example, if you worked for Nokia and you're applying for a job with Motorola's cell phone division, emphasize that your background is in the same area of expertise:

- Five years of user interface, with four on mobile phones

If the industry you're applying for matches part of your background, then call attention to that. Applying in the real estate? Then maybe your background in the financial industry is worth noting:

- Seven years Windows network administration for New York investment banks.

Anything you can do that shows that you are a good match for the target employer is worth highlighting. Hiring managers will tend to hire people familiar with the specific situation being hired for. Here are some other examples of similarities you may be able to draw attention to:

- Tools used
- Industry worked in
- Types of users supported (Artists? Accountants? Executives?)
- Geographic area worked
- Size of company
- Size of department
- Size of team

Don't forget who you're selling this résumé to. Even something as basic as your summary of experience may vary depending on the target of the résumé. What may be an unnecessary detail in one scenario may be what catches the eye of a hiring manager in another. You must know your target.

Main Expertise

Your expertise is where you explain your top technical skills, quantifiably if possible. Be as specific as you can, unless your expertise is that your knowledge is broad. For example, it might be one of these:

- Extensive work with Ruby, including two years of Rails
- Expert Solaris sysadmin, supporting more than 200 work-stations
- Managed work teams of three to eight developers and testers
- Three years experience writing 100-to-300-page manuals with FrameMaker
- Tested software on platforms from Red Hat Linux to Mac OS X to Windows XP
- Taught more than ten different training classes to groups of up to 100 students

Note how each of these is brief, quantifiable, and specific.

Other Expertise

You may have other areas of expertise that are worth mentioning, maybe only for a specific target company. Examples might include the following:

- Fluent in Spanish, including some error message translation
- Active in open source development, including acting as Perl 6 project manager
- Extensive experience with gravel pit management software

> An objective is a waste of prime résumé real estate.

What if you're fresh out of school and don't have professional experience? Some books say that you can use an objective instead of a professional summary if you don't have an extensive background, but I disagree. An objective makes *your* wants most prominent, rather than what you can do to help the *employer's* needs. Instead, turn your school or hobby experience into summary bullet points, and add one bullet for the direction you'd like to go. For example:

- Recent graduate of Illinois Institute of Technology, computer science major, with 3.43 GPA
- Two years of work on open source projects, including Perl 6 and Ruby on Rails
- Frequent leader of class projects, from two to six students
- Looking to work for a small startup or with music and audio recording

This final bullet may smell like the dreaded objective, but in this case, some sort of directional statement is important, because the hiring company won't know where you're going.

Double-check your synopsis. Does it stand alone? With nothing else on your résumé but your name, email address, and synopsis, could you see getting an interview? If so, you have a strong synopsis.

Work Experience

Your past work experience is the best predictor of future job performance, and that's what you'll explain next. The work experience should be the largest part of your résumé, unless you've never had a relevant job before.

Here's the rough outline form of your work experience section:

```
Conglomerated Frobbitz, Inc., Lincoln, NE (2005-present)
CFI is a leading distributor of replacement parts for widgetrons.

    Lead software architect (2007-present)
    * Led team of five creating framework for testing of software.
       This framework became the standard testing tool for CFI,
       testing more than 6M lines of code daily.
    * Established requirements for...
    ...

    Programmer (2005-2007)
    * Coded and testing widgetron design software in Java as part
       of team of seven.
    * Built command-line tools to....

Feed Lot Solutions, Milford, NE (2004-2005)
FLS produces farm management software for feed lots in the US,
Canada, and Australia.

    Programmer
    * Designed forms and coded business in Visual Basic for core
       product, CowTracker Plus
```

```
    * Instituted bug tracking software to replace ad hoc Excel
       spreadsheets that FLS had been using
    ....

Southeast Community College, Milford, NE (2002-2004)

    Computer lab assistant
    * Answered technical questions about...
    * Helped first-year programming students with...
```

The company heading is simple: name of the company, where it is, and when you worked there. If the company is a large one, specify a branch or division to let the reader have some idea of what your work group did. If you worked at General Electric, don't leave the reader wondering if you worked on lightbulbs or aircraft engines. If the company is unlikely to be familiar with the reader, then it's nice to include a short description of the company to give a flavor to your background. This can be left out only if you're short on space, if the target company is in the same industry, or if they're widely known.

> Your résumé is not a
> reference sheet.

Note that you are not including information such as phone numbers, street addresses, or any of your contacts at the company. Don't try to make your résumé do double duty as your reference sheet. You may, if the website is relevant to the job search, include the company's URL. Don't bother if the company is well-known.

List the dates of employment for the position, but don't waste space by including the months. If you're still working, leave the ending year off or say "(2007-present)." Certainly don't say why you left the position on the résumé. I've seen people write things like "(2002-2004, company downsized)." That downsizing information isn't relevant to your skills, so leave it out. If an interviewer wants to know why you left a company, she'll ask.

The bullets underneath each company tell what you accomplished at the company:

```
Position: System administrator
* Managed 150-seat, 10-server Windows network infrastructure,
   including Exchange Server and Microsoft SQL Server.
* Provided second-tier technical support for the help desk.
* Created disaster recovery plans and upgraded old backup plans.
```

The Power of Open Source to Your Career

Open source software projects not only power much of the Internet, but they can give a boost to your career, especially when you're just starting out. They can also give you that important experience and sample work to give as you start your job search.

Working on an open source software (OSS) project, either your own or an existing project, *is real work experience*. It shows that you're able to create code, work on a team, and get along with others. It leaves a trail on the Web that an employer will be able to find and see.

Open source project work also gives you real examples of your skills that you are free to show to anyone. At conferences, after I say to bring a portfolio of work to interviews (see Section 7.4, *Prepare a Relevant Portfolio*, on page 125), someone will always complain with this: "I can't show samples of my work, because all the code I write is proprietary." That's too bad, because it puts them at a disadvantage. OSS is an ideal solution, because it's a way to show your chops publicly.

Your contributions need not be large, and they might not even be code. You can contribute documentation, add pages to the project wiki, or just answer questions on a mailing list. The key is that you're giving back value on real programming projects in a demonstrable way.

If you're not involved in open source yet, find a project that interests you today. Visit Google Code* or Source-Forge,† two huge repositories of open source projects. Your career will thank you.

---

*. http://code.google.com/
†. http://sourceforge.net

* Specified, planned, and rolled out Active Directory integration across the enterprise.
* Established and reached service levels of 99.99% uptime.
* Created dedicated Linux backup server with Quantum tape backup unit. This reduced human backup costs by 80%.

Start by explaining what position you held at the company. If you had an official title, use it on the résumé, because the hiring company may call to check your employment history at your old company and may be concerned if the titles don't match. If your title is vague, like when I was once a "Member of Technical Staff," you may want to parenthetically add your own description of the position, like "Member of Technical Staff (product release manager)."

Highlight advancement by listing different positions.

If you've held two radically different positions at a company, don't try to combine them into one section. Repeat this section for each position. You want your advancement or job shift to stand out and to tell the story. In the previous example, the résumé's author started as a programmer and became a lead software architect. That's a big jump in responsibilities and should be highlighted.

This is also the case if you changed the type of work in a lateral move. For instance, you might list 2001–2003 for programmer and 2003–2005 for sysadmin, even if they were both at the same level of responsibility.

Your bullet list for the position should give interesting, useful information about the work you performed and benefits that you brought to the company. Write short, punchy sentences that describe actions. Don't say "I did this, I did that," because the reader knows who the subject of the sentence is.

Note how the bullets in the example go from the general to the specific, from the most important to the least important. This is just like everything else on your résumé. Each bullet gives a specific description of the work being done, using the active voice. Each bullet uses an active verb to describe what was done. You say you "provided support," not "was the help desk guy." Describe it in terms of what you did, not what you were.

How many bullets should you have? It varies widely, depending on how much responsibility you had, how far back the position was, and how relevant to your current position it was. Your most recent job should probably have at least four to six bullets unless you were there for a very short time. On the other hand, my first full-time programming job back in 1986 gets two bullet points at the tail end of my résumé.

Coming up with your bullets is the toughest part of the entire résumé process. I recommend that you start it early; just scribble ideas on a sheet of paper that you carry with you. Don't worry about order or phrasing at this early phase. Write down everything you can remember doing, and worry about pruning later. It's far easier to get rid of extra information than to come up with one more bullet at the last minute.

Résumé books often talk about the importance of using "action words" in your bullet points. They'll list pages of words you can use in your résumé to **Focus on the story, not specific buzzwords.** sound like you were effective: analyzed, compiled, coordinated, drafted, devised, implemented, blah blah blah. Although it's true that you want to use active verbs, as I noted earlier, don't get hung up on which snazzy word you use. Instead, focus on the details of the work, getting as specific as possible.

Details include numbers. If you can quantify some value that comes from the work you did, it gives weight to the value that provided. Even if you weren't the only person working on a project, you can still discuss your involvement. Here are some examples:

- Increased traffic to website 50% over six months by (and list the actions you took to make it happen)
- Led teams of four to six programmers
- Created new task tracking system that reduced schedule creep by 40%
- Installed new routers that increased throughput 25%, virtually eliminating the 20% of help desk calls related to network responsiveness
- Reduced open ticket backlog from 500 to 20 in three months.

- Refactored codebase to take advantage of standard C++ libraries, reducing total LOC from 100,000 to 70,000

> **Quantifiable claims are powerful.**

Quantifiable claims are of particular interest to an interviewer and will likely be discussed in the interview. Make sure that you can back up the numbers you're claiming, and don't fudge. If you must use an estimate, make it clear that it is an estimate, and give the source of the estimate: "Implemented a new asset tracking system. The warehouse manager estimated this reduced paperwork by 75%."

Where possible, specify numbers as percentages and trends rather than absolute numbers. Saying "increased web traffic by 10,000 hits/day" doesn't give any sense of scale, but "increased web traffic by 40%" does. Also specify time spans. "Increased website traffic by 40%" doesn't specify the time it took to make the change and leaves the reader wondering. In a week? A year? The timeframe makes a difference.

But what if you don't know the numbers? Then you'll have to do without but with much less impact. Take this opportunity now to remember to update your résumé with metrics like this as often as possible. (See more about using your résumé as a résumé tracking tool in Chapter 12, *Staying Hirable*, on page 215.)

Value for the Employer

As you create bullets for each position, emphasize actions you took or were involved in that improved the company, the department, or the product. Even in the most mundane of positions, chances are you did *something* to improve things.

I was working with my friend Kirrily Robert to revise her long and varied résumé. In all jobs but one, she listed ways that she had improved things, whether creating coding standards or being a one-woman system administration department. One job, however, stuck out. The two short bullets describing it were bland and uninteresting.

Andy: *I'd be more comfortable if this position somehow tied to business value. Were you designing stuff from the ground up?*

The Guy Who Drove the Mosquito Truck

One common bit of wrong-headed advice is that gaps in your employment history are poison. I once got a résumé where the first job in the candidate's work history, an inch of the most valuable visual real estate on his résumé, was driving the mosquito spray truck for his town. He had more than a decade of programming experience, but apparently he'd been unable to find a job for two years. I guess he figured I wouldn't see a gap in his employment history if he put down that he was the mosquito truck driver. In fact, you don't need to explain employment gaps in your résumé. If an interviewer is interested in details, she'll ask at the interview.

He'd also apparently read the common knowledge that you must always use action words to describe your job responsibilities, with descriptions like "Precisely followed planned routes to deliver proper amount of spray" and "Accurately logged all activities."

Although it's true that you always want to show how you provided value to your employer, the ability to follow routes and keep logs is not one that I, hiring a programmer, am at all interested in. I certainly don't want to see it as the first thing on a résumé. Employers understand that sometimes it's hard to get a job, and if you have to drive the mosquito truck or sell appliances at Sears to make ends meet until your next programming job, so be it. Just don't make us read about it.

Kirrily: Nah, it was maintenance and the odd new feature. All very back end and unsexy I'm afraid.

Andy: Did you do anything cool at that job? Inflict coding standards? Set up bug tracking?

Kirrily: Nope and nope. Managed to write some automated tests.

Andy: Did they have any before you started there?

Kirrily: Yes, just not good ones. They spat out reams of text you had to parse for yourself, and Perl's Test::Harness couldn't run them properly. I finally got them to run right.

Andy: *Aha! So you "overhauled the automated unit test suite to conform to the Perl testing standards." There's your improvement.*

Note how with a bit of digging, we turned up a valuable bit of her background that would have gone unmentioned. That one bullet now shows the résumé reader that Kirrily understands unit testing and Perl's testing framework and that she has a nose for improvement.

Education

The basics of the "Education" section are to show the names of the institutions of higher education you've attended and the degrees received at each. You can also list individual courses of interest and your GPA if it's worth noting.

> Master of Computer Science (emphasis on algorithms),
>   University of Chicago, 2002
> Bachelor of Arts, American Literature, Poughkeepsie College, 1998

Note that we're talking about "higher education," which means "not high school." Employers assume you've completed high school, so you need not specify that you have, or have not, done so. In fact, listing your high-school education only draws attention to your not having college. You especially don't want to include anything about high school if you only have a GED (General Equivalency Diploma).

If you're currently working toward a degree, treat it with the expectation that you'll be graduating on time:

> Bachelor of Science, Scranton Technical Institute, 2010
> (anticipated)

If you don't have any degrees, you can still list schools you've attended and classes you've taken. Maybe you're just starting to work on a degree. List relevant courses you've taken.

> Working toward an Associate of Science in Management degree from McHenry County College by taking evening classes. Courses taken include Principles of Management, Management Theory in Practice, and three semesters of Business Accounting.

Other forms of education may be relevant as well. Perhaps you took a week-long training class in systems administration. That's certainly worth putting in your "Education" section. However, if it was part of your certification process, put it in your "Certifications" section, as I'll discuss in the next section.

Keep certification classes under "Certifications," not "Education."

Training courses:

- Principles of Web Security, 2006, three-day training course from TechShield Education
- Extreme Programming: A Week Hands-On, 2005, five-day lecture/lab from XP Partners

If you have no college work at all, and no relevant education, just leave the "Education" section out entirely, and use that space to tell other wonderful things about yourself. How much you emphasize your education, both in terms of amount of detail and positioning on the page, may depend on the company you're applying for. A Silicon Valley startup may be far less interested in your degrees than a research institution or indeed any educational institution. On the other hand, what if that institution is a prestigious one like MIT? The nature of the job may also be relevant. A high-level planning and research position may need more emphasis on education than an entry-level system administrator.

Certifications

Certifications can be an efficient, accepted way of showing that you've achieved a level of proficiency in your chosen area, or they can be useless noise that make it look like you're trying to be more impressive than you really are. The key is for you to know the difference.

In some areas, like Microsoft-heavy shops, having certification as a Microsoft Certified Systems Engineer (MCSE), the predecessor to MCITP, carries a lot of weight, if not actually being a hiring requirement. I've seen many MCSEs put it in their contact block, as in "Bob Smith, MCSE," and include a little graphic from Microsoft that says they're properly certified. The Microsoft certifications are well-respected in that sector of the computing world, so it makes sense to play them up. If you're hiring for a sysadmin in a Windows shop, it probably makes sense to put a "Certifications" section above your "Education" section and maybe even your "Professional Experience" section. The same would hold true if you have a generally accepted certification, such as a CCNA or CCNE from Cisco.

On the other hand, applying for a position at an all-Unix shop, where they like to say that MCSE stands for Minesweeper-Certified Solitaire Expert, you'd give less weight to that MCSE. It's still relevant as an achievement in your background but of less relevance to the employer. You'd probably want to move it down in importance on the résumé.

Finally, some certifications don't carry much weight at all. For example, there are no generally accepted certifications for Perl programmers. Nonetheless, I'll see people cite having been certified as "scoring 92 percent in Perl at SomeTestingSite.com," where the site is one of those offering poorly written tests apparently written by freelancers skimming a language manual.

 Make sure you can back up your certifications and education. I'll see expertise mentioned in "Certifications" or "Education," but without experience on the résumé to back it up. That smells like a résumé author trying to show that he's something he's not. If you're going to make claims about yourself with certifications, make sure you understand what you're claiming. If not, leave it out.

 Finally, don't list hokey online societies and classes that offer negligible value. Don't list yourself as a member of the HTML Writers Guild, for example, when all it takes to be a member is $40/year.

Honors, Awards, Activities, and Memberships

A section on awards and honors can be a great way to highlight some of your achievements that don't fit into any other headings. It's also likely to be read because it's there, just like the "P.S." at the end of advertising letters.

Professional awards may include an honor bestowed by an organization, such as the SourceForge Community Choice Awards for outstanding open source software, or one given by your company, such as the Acme Corporation Leadership in Action award. Unless the award is widely known, it's worth explaining the honor in a line below the bullet.

Don't list an award unless it is special and meaningful. If the Leadership in Action award is given to only three people in the 10,000-person corporation, then it's quite an honor. However, if it's "awarded" to anyone with 90 percent or better attendance, then it's hardly special. Chances are you'll be asked about these awards and honors during the interview, so make sure you don't list something where you'll look foolish trying to explain why it's an honor to receive it.

Academic examples include making the dean's list or being awarded a scholarship. List the year or years in which the honor was awarded. In the case of a scholarship, do not list the dollar amount of the scholarship.

For professional activities, you can list groups of which you're a member. Even when referring to well-known groups like the Association for Computing Machinery (ACM), spell out the full name. Don't list the HTML Writers' Guild, and *please* don't list your World of Warcraft clan, even if coordinating weekly dungeon raids requires organizational skills.[2]

Awards

- Dean's List, 2002–2003
- Microracle Technical Scholarship, 2005

Honors

- White Camel award, The Perl Foundation, 2005 One of 3 given for outstanding service to the Perl community

Whatever you put in this section, make sure they're meaningful. Remember back in the late 1990s when websites had absurd badges saying the site was deemed "Top 5% of the Web," whatever that meant? That's what you want to avoid.

---

2. I swear I am not making up this example. See http://beyond-summit.blogspot.com/2006/09/would-you-put-wow-on-your-resume.html.

Other Achievements

Listing outside achievements can be a great way to show that there's more to you than your core skills, but *only if you have limited experience.* If you're fresh out of school or have been working for only a few years, then you may need to turn to non-work activities to show your skills. If you have a good solid working background, then outside achievements will just be noise.

List outside achievements only if your work experience is weak.

If you do decide to list achievements, then remember that you are showing "achievements," not "things I like to do." Say you're a fan of renaissance faires. Dressing up at the ren faire every weekend isn't an achievement, but acting as treasurer for East Poughkeepsie Renaissance Faire Fans is. Turn it into an example of your skills and how you'll help the company, like so:

Outside activities:

Treasurer, East Poughkeepsie Renaissance Faire Fans (2004–present)

- Responsible for all cash flow and tracking of accounts for this 501(c)(3) nonprofit organization.
- Created yearly accounts of all monies per U.S. law.

Even if 99 percent of the money involved with the running of the East Poughkeepsie Renaissance Faire Geeks is collecting dues throughout the year and buying beer for the midwinter beer bash, you're showing responsibility and financial savvy that may count for something in the eyes of the reader.

Here are some ideas to get you thinking how to present them.

Instead of...	Say This...
I like painting.	Self-taught painter with oils and watercolors. My piece "Night In a Cave" won third place in the 2004 Boston Cavalcade of the Arts.
I like playing chess.	I'm an avid chess player. When I left Stanford in 2002, I was the fifth-ranked player in the All-Campus Chess League.

Instead of...	Say This...
I like rock climbing.	Rock climbing is a passion. The group I helped organize, Flatlander Rock Climbers, is going on our first expedition to the Painted Desert in Arizona in March 2010.
I play banjo.	I've played banjo since I was eight. I play with the local Dixieland band Fireball Eight, where we play McHenry Fiesta Days each year.

In each of these cases, they may not be huge achievements, but they show that you apply yourself in your hobbies. As always, it's a matter of selling yourself and bringing to light what you have to offer.

Remember with topics not directly related to your job responsibilities that it may cross the line into Too Much Information, as discussed in Section 10.2, *Other Topics to Avoid*, on page 187. Treasurer for the local ren faire group may be innocuous, but treasurer for the local chapter of Greenpeace or the National Rifle Association may put off the reader. Balance the risk with the rewards.

Buzzwords and Skills

Somewhere near the bottom of your résumé, include a section of a list of skills and buzzwords that you know. This list exists only to appease automated keyword checkers and human résumé screeners unfamiliar with your area of expertise. It also helps your online footprint so that people searching the Web or a company's résumé database will be more likely to find your résumé.

Say you've got a bullet point in your "Experience" section like this:

- Created applications for company intranet such as phone listings and in-house repair tracking using Perl, the Catalyst framework, and an Oracle back end.

That gives the high-level view but doesn't fill in as many buzzwords as possible. If you're writing in Perl to a database, you're using *DBI* and other *CPAN modules* and writing *SQL* queries. You need not explain that level of detail in the "Experience" section, but you can now include bullets in your "Buzzwords" section like this:

- Perl: CPAN modules, DBI, Mason
- Databases: Oracle, SQL

Now if someone is searching the Web for "résumé Perl SQL," she'll get a hit on your résumé. Without your "Buzzwords" section, your résumé would not have been found. Many companies may have human screeners who do the same thing. The hiring manager may say "I gotta have someone who knows Perl and can write SQL." To you, it's obvious that if you're using Oracle, you're writing SQL, but to the HR clerk, it's not.

Put as much detail as is relevant into your buzzword bullets. Details help reinforce your credibility and give the reader a better feel for what you know. For example, rather than say you have experience administering "Windows servers," specify "administered Windows NT, Windows 2000, and Windows 2003 servers." Note how I've spelled out each version of Windows, instead of saying "Windows NT, 2000, and 2003," so that someone searching for "Windows 2000" will match that string.

On the other hand, irrelevant details are a nuisance and make the list harder to read. If you're just saying that you're proficient with Windows as a user, specify only "Windows XP" and not the older versions. Nobody cares if you've been a Windows user since Windows 3.1.

How do you know when to be detailed and when to cut it short? If it relates to your core skills, then give details. If it's merely a side part of your knowledge, be sparse. A programmer might make mention of knowing how to use Microsoft Project, but a project manager would be wise to specify versions of Project she's worked with.

One of the places I see people go overboard the most is in listing Unix-like operating systems they've worked on. For most programmer positions, specifying that you're comfortable with Linux and Solaris is enough, but I've seen people list individual Linux distributions (Ubuntu, Debian, Red Hat, Slackware) and even versions of distributions (Slackware 8.1, 8.2, and 9)! On the other hand, for a system administrator, this may make sense. On the third hand, at the time of this writing, Ubuntu is white-hot, and a programmer might be wise to make mention of it in her résumé. Bottom line: consider the audience for this specific résumé.

A final note: I suggest you label this section "Buzzwords," because it shows that you're aware that it is an artifact of the keyword index-driven nature of the job world. If the thought of a résumé with a "Buzzwords" section horrifies you, you might go with "Detailed Skills List." Whatever term you use, make it clear that it's not required reading.

Can I Have Other Sections?

Absolutely! The Résumé Police will not be knocking on the door if you add something outside the standard "Education," "Experience," and "Achievement" sections. On my own résumé, I have sections for "Publishing," about various books I've worked on; "Open Source," where I list projects I've worked on; and "Presentations & Papers," for talks I've given at conferences and user groups. None of those would fit neatly into "Experience," so why try to shoehorn them in?

Branch out a little! Give the reader something interesting to remember from your résumé. Maybe you wrote some software on the side, so add a "Software Written" section. How about a section called "Why I Love Programming," listing your top five bullets about what you love about your profession? Whatever section you add should look like a section so as to be clear that it's not a continuation of the section preceding it, but beyond that, put in whatever you want.

What Order Should the Sections Go In?

Put the most important and impressive section, *as it relates to the job you're applying for*, as the first section after your summary.

Is your education the best part of your background? Put that up first. If instead your work experience is your strongest asset, then put that up first. Temper that with what the employer may find to be most important. If you're applying to work for a school or university, you may want to put education first. What if you went to MIT instead of McHenry County College? If you're applying to work for the Free Software Foundation, you might have a section called "Free Software Work" before anything else. The only Résumé Police is the recipient of the résumé.

3.4 What to Leave Out of Your Résumé

When people copy from other résumés without thinking about it, they carry around baggage that doesn't make sense to include, simply because they saw someone else do it. Every word on your résumé must have value and not detract from the rest. Here's a partial list of what to leave out.

Anything You Can't Be Asked in an Interview

There are topics that U.S. law prevents an employer from asking you about in an interview, such as religious affiliations and national origin. Chapter 10, *Too Much Information*, on page 183 covers these in depth. If you can't be asked about it in your interview, don't put it in your résumé.

Photo

In many European countries, it's common to attach a small photo of yourself to your résumé. In the United States, don't do it. It has no bearing on your job, and unless you're applying to be a model, it's not a job qualification.

An Objective

An objective is the worst thing to have at the top of your résumé. It's in the most important real estate of your résumé, and it's filled with information that belongs in your cover letter, is redundant to the rest of the résumé, or has no meaning whatsoever.[3] Here's a sample objective from someone who thinks they need an objective but no idea why:

> OBJECTIVE: To acquire a challenging position in the field of information technology and to contribute my skills to business development.

This objective says mostly nothing, and what it does say is self-serving. The very word *objective* says, "This is what I want,"

---

3. You'll read more about how to write an effective cover letter in Section 6.2, *Create a Cover Letter*, on page 112.

rather than how the writer can help the reader's company. Everyone wants a "challenging position," and it's obvious it's "in the field of information technology" if you're applying for an IT job. It's so vague it sounds like the writer will take any job in IT.

Here's an excerpt from another objective from an actual résumé:

> "I am confident that my experience and education, coupled with an eagerness to learn and a motivation to succeed, would contribute to a productive association with your company."

The writer says "my experience and education," which is redundant to the rest of the résumé. Stock phrases like "eagerness to learn" and "motivation to succeed" are the résumé equivalent of "enjoy long walks on the beach" in a personal ad.[4]

Worst of all, the statement is baseless. How can the writer be "confident that my experience...would contribute to a productive association?" The writer probably knows next to nothing about the specific needs of the company to which he sent the résumé, so how can he have this confidence?

The one case that I could see having an objective is when you don't know where you'll be showing your résumé. For example, if you're relatively new in your career and you'll be handing out dozens of résumés without cover letters at a job fair, some people say an objective can help the recruiter remember what direction you're looking to go. In that case, incorporate it into your professional summary as detailed in Section 3.3, *The Professional Summary*, on page 40.

Lists of Hobbies and Interests

Usually these come out as "Interests: music and reading." Whoop-de-do, everyone likes music and reading. If you feel that your hobbies are somehow related to the job or will give you some kind of "geek cred," then create a section on your résumé for non-work-related achievements, as described in Section 3.3, *Other Achievements*, on page 56. Simply listing your hobbies is not useful.

---

4. See Appendix A, on page 235, for more of these empty filler phrases to avoid.

"References Available Upon Request"

The worst example of "cargo-cult" résumé writing, where people do what they've seen on other résumés without thinking about why they're doing it, is putting "References available upon request" at the bottom of the résumé. It's unnecessary to say, and it takes up valuable space and visual real estate.

Every hiring manager assumes that you'll have some references to provide when the time comes in the hiring process (and see Section 11.4, *Give Solid References*, on page 197 for how to do that). You need not worry that someone reading your résumé will say "Jenkins here looks good on paper, but she doesn't have references available upon request."

Irrelevant Work Experience

My first real job was at a McDonald's at age 16. It doesn't help me as a programmer, so I leave it off my résumé. The only reason to put unrelated work experience on your résumé is if you're just starting out and it's your *only* work experience. See also the sidebar on page 51 for another tale of irrelevance.

Consider carefully what you consider irrelevant. If you're applying to be a systems administrator, a job as a hardware engineer is probably relevant, but you'd want to leave out your experience as a chef. However, if you were looking to be a team lead for programmers, that experience as a chef, managing a group of people, would certainly be worth noting. Don't bother with the technical details of the kitchen experience, but do look at what analogs exist with the job you're applying for.

Also, "irrelevant" is not the same as "outdated." You may have started writing Apple Pascal code on an Apple II in the mid-80s, but that's worth a couple lines at the bottom of your résumé to show the breadth and duration of your experience. However, list it only within the context of the position and without going into too much detail.

3.5 Moving to Construction

By now, you should have a good idea of what you'll be including in your base résumé. You've identified what you'll be listing in each of the major sections of your résumé, and you should have some idea of how they support each other.

You're thinking in terms of sales value, in letting the reader know who you are and what makes you special. You're comfortable writing about your achievements, and you have achievements on the brain, because that's all that matters. You're also keeping an eye out for anything that doesn't help move you toward getting the interest of a hiring manager at your future employer. Omit needless words!

You probably also have some other notes, bullets, and text that didn't feel right in your base résumé but you don't want to throw away. Perhaps you have a scraps.txt file in your résumé directory. You know your résumé will change for each job you pursue, although the basic framework will probably be the same, so you're keeping notes and ideas for when they might come up.

With all the building blocks of your résumé at hand, move forward to résumé construction.

Chapter 4

Building Your Résumé Documents

In the previous chapter, we looked at the textual content of your résumé. You should have a decent collection of text and notes that you want to let your future employer know about you. You should have a good idea of the order of importance and what you want to emphasize. Now it's time to put the pieces together.

Keep four basic rules in mind when building your résumé:

- It is your first work product for your new company.
- It will be seen by more people than you expect.
- It must be perfect.
- Presentation is content.

Your résumé gives each reader an impression of the type of work you can do and the pride you take in that work. Lack of pride in the work you've done

Your résumé is a work product.

will show. You're in a technical, detail-oriented industry, and your résumé and attention to detail must reflect that if you're to show yourself as a detail-oriented worker.

In addition, use the specific tools properly. Use Word as a word processor, not just a fancier version of Notepad. Show that you're able to use HTML properly if you're at all involved with the Web. If your résumé says that you create neat, clean C++ and Java code but your HTML code is ugly slop, you undermine your message.

In our industry, the document isn't just what prints on the paper or renders in a browser window, but the entire electronic file. Show that you're a power user of the tools at your command. If you think that no one will look at the internals of your document, think again. Maybe nobody in HR will, but there's a good chance that someone in a more technical role will.

Finally, if you're one of those people who thinks of "content" as different from "presentation," now is the time to disabuse yourself of that notion for the sake of both your résumé and your career. Don't think that because you're interested in a programming job that visual design is irrelevant. Presentation *is* content, and your résumé is more than just the words contained on it. If it weren't, magazines would all use monospaced typewriter fonts, and we'd still be using Gopher instead of the Web. The text in your résumé may be perfect, but if it's unattractively presented, people are less likely to read it.

4.1 The Three Versions of Your Résumé

Plan on making three versions of your résumé: one in Word, one in plain text, and an HTML version for your website. It's nice to send PDFs of your Word documents if that's an option for an employer, but I've never seen a job ad that required a résumé in PDF.

"Aw, man," I hear some of you saying, "three formats?" Yes, you're going to have to be able to send off a copy in Word when it's asked for. You're also going to want a copy in plain text to send to companies that don't want attachments or if you're posting into a little web form on some job site. Finally, you'll want a copy up on your website for Google and all other search engines to find.

Some of you may hate Microsoft and hate Word documents. Richard Stallman has written extensively about how he thinks that Word documents limit freedom.[1] You may even agree with his ideas. The pragmatic job hunter will set this aside.

---

1. See his "We Can Put an End to Word Documents" at http://www.gnu.org/philosophy/no-word-attachments.htm

Most places you'll apply to will ask for a résumé in Word format. They probably find it easiest to deal with or have a process that relies on Word documents. Maybe it's automated software that scans for keywords. Who knows? All that matters is that companies ask for Word documents, and your job is to give them what they ask for. Use OpenOffice if you like, available for free.[2] It will generate documents in Word format, and you won't have to soil your computer with Microsoft code.

If a potential employer asks for Word and you send a PDF or a text file, you've told him this: "I am unable to follow directions on my first assignment." Don't second-guess your future hiring manager or presume to know better how things should be done. Don't let your personal preferences over software usage scuttle your chance at a job.

If you find Word to be such an odious file format and you think that any company that requires its use in a résumé is run by idiots, then you and that company are not a good match. Don't bother sending the résumé. Move on to another option.

4.2 General Guidelines

Some rules apply regardless of the format you're writing. Here are some to keep in mind.

Your name must be the first thing the reader notices and can easily find. If you have any multipage documents, your name and contact information must appear on each page. Your name should be the biggest thing in the contact block. Use a strong sans serif typeface, and put your name in bold and a few point sizes bigger than the rest of the contact information. You want it to stand out on a stack of papers. Whether it's left- or right-justified doesn't much matter, as long as your name is on the top.

Use exactly two fonts. Use a sans-serif font like Tahoma, Arial, or Geneva for your headings, and use a serif font like Times New Roman for everything else.

Font choice is not the place to get creative.

---

2. http://openoffice.org

Keep your body text at a size between 9 and 12 points and slightly larger for headings. Some say, "I like sans-serif for body text better; I think it looks nicer," but this most basic rule of typography still holds. Take a look at this book you're reading right now if you don't believe me.

When you choose fonts, choose common ones that are likely to be on the recipient's machine. You may have a stunning sans serif font that is just perfect in your headings, but it won't matter when the reader opens a Word document and gets a "Could not find font Astrocardigan Sans" dialog box. The reader's web browser will not even ask and will replace the fonts you lovingly chose with its best guess. Unless you're printing out a document on paper, stick with the boring but ubiquitous standbys like Times New Roman, Arial, and Tahoma.

Don't justify your paragraphs. Justification is when your word processor adjusts spacing between words to make each line of a paragraph the same length as the others, giving a smooth right margin. Look at the lines in this paragraph for an example. In books you want justified margins, but there's nothing wrong with a ragged right margin in a résumé. Justifying may make your word processor introduce weird spacing artifacts. Definitely do not try to justify a text-only document in a fixed-width font.

Spell everything perfectly. Be especially careful with acronyms. Know when to use capitalization and periods. For example, Java and Perl are not acronyms and are not spelled JAVA and PERL. Misspellings other than case also mean that your keywords won't get properly indexed by automated résumé software. Spell out acronyms on first use unless they're well-known enough to stand on their own (IIS, SQL, HTML).

Don't use all capitals, even in headings. It's enough to make a heading of "McHenry Tool & Die" without making it "MCHENRY TOOL & DIE." The problem is not that all caps is seen as shouting, as the old email canard goes, but that it's not correct written English.

Don't put any graphics in your résumé, with the exception of badges related to your certifications, and then only if the certification is a key part of your qualifications. If you've earned the right to display a certification logo and you're looking for a job where that's a primary qualification, then go ahead and include it in your résumé, probably as part of or near the summary. Other than that, leave the graphics out. They're just noise.

Consider the overall visual impact of your résumé. Think about what the reader will see as a whole. What words appear immediately? Your name should be immediately obvious, as well as who you are.

4.3 Use Word's Features Correctly and Effectively

Most of your time should be spent on the Word document. It's probably the one that most people will be seeing and that you'll fuss over the most. Consider the Word version of your résumé to be the master. However, it's likely there may be detailed information on the HTML version of your résumé that you keep on your website that won't fit on the printed Word résumé. On mine, these include open source projects I've worked on, presentations I've given, and articles and books I've worked on. This would be too much detail for the print version, but on the Web you can stretch out a bit.

I'm not going to explain the details of using Word or OpenOffice in this chapter. I'll assume that you're able to make your way around one of the most commonly used software packages in the world.

Don't use the résumé templates that ship with Word. They violate many of my rules, such as including objectives and using sans serif typefaces for body content. However, the document files themselves are good examples of how to use named styles, discussed in a moment.

Here are Word-specific guidelines to follow.

Use Named Styles

Just as in HTML pages where you don't want to use presentation markup when you can use CSS, you should use Word's named styles feature. You need not limit yourself to the styles that Word provides, although they make sense to look at. Using named styles also encourages a consistent look across your entire résumé, so you won't be tempted to make body text in "Experience" be a different font than body text in "Education."

Use Tab Stops, Not Spaces

Word uses tab stops for positioning elements. When you hit Tab, Word positions you to the next tab stop, which may or may not be a half inch in from where your cursor was. Each tab position can be left- or right-justified or centered. You can set tab stops for a given style in the Format Style dialog, but more likely you'll use what Word gives you.

Use the Spell Checker

Make sure that the spell-check-as-you-type feature is turned on. Think of it as unit testing for your words, and the sooner you discover a bug in a sentence, the better. Misspellings are the easiest way to get your résumé ignored, so take advantage of the tool. It's not the only tool, though. You'll still need to use your eyes, and those of other people, to ensure you have no typos.

Use the Header/Footer Feature

Multipage résumés have a way of getting their printed pages separated. Your résumé needs contact information on every page, and Word's headers feature lets you do it easily and consistently. Let Word worry about where the page breaks fall.

When entering information in the header of your résumé, be sure to use the preset tab stops to let Word take care of the flush right margin.

4.4 Create an Effective Summary

The summary is where you'll be grabbing the reader's eye. Start with the bullets you wrote back in Section 3.3, *The Professional Summary*, on page 40, using Word's List Bullet style. Don't give the summary a heading, because it's obvious what it is.

Here's an example of a summary that boils down the qualifications to the most important high points, with little detail:

• Seven years' experience in all facets of large website production.

- Led team of five designers creating Flash content for automotive websites.

- Installed and maintained content management systems such as Vignette and Bricolage for production staff of 20.

- Accomplished author of technical documentation in French. Also fluent in Japanese.

Now, call attention to the most important words. Set them in **bold** to jump out at the reader. Consider which are the most important words for the reader to know about you in the first few seconds of looking at your résumé.

- **Seven years'** experience in all facets of **large website production**.

- **Led team of five** designers creating Flash content for automotive websites.

- Installed and maintained **content management systems** such as **Vignette** and **Bricolage** for production staff of 20.

- Accomplished author of **technical documentation in French**. Also **fluent in Japanese**.

Note how the words are exactly the same, but the bolding of the keywords draws the reader to what's most important, helping her to the really good parts. You're trying to grab attention and to do it legitimately.

Don't overdo the bold, or you'll turn everything a mass of dark blobs. In the previous example, if you were applying to a company that specialized in the automotive industry, you might bold **automotive websites** in favor of other keywords in that bullet. As with everything, it all depends on the target company and the specific job.

4.5 Check Your Word Document

Before you do any other check, run a spell check on your résumé. Even if you don't make mistakes, even if you've had as-you-type spell checking turned on the whole time, run a spell check anyway. It'll take just a few seconds and may save you from getting your résumé thrown away.

What About Pink Paper?

You want your résumé to get noticed and to get read by the hiring manager. Some conventional wisdom says that it's a good idea to use noticeable paper, like pink or orange, so that your résumé shows up in a stack of résumés and is more likely to be read. It's not. It just makes the reader think you're a chump for believing that bit of conventional un-wisdom.

When you print your résumé to bring to the interview, print it on white, off-white, or cream-colored paper. You can get nice résumé paper at the local office store. Use black ink or toner.

You've done all the typing there is to do for now. It's not enough for your Word document to look good on the screen. It has to look good on paper and has to be able to make the trip to paper, as well. I've received countless résumés where the candidate looked interesting enough that I wanted to print out the résumé, and when I did, I got warnings about the document not fitting on the page, or the page breaks would be wrong and one page would creep over to another. Don't let it happen to you. Print the document, and look at it on paper, just as you hope the hiring manager will.

Here's how I do it:

1. Print the document on your printer.
2. Get a red pen to get in a high school English mind-set.
3. Go far away from the computer to get a fresh perspective.
4. Scrutinize for errors. Imagine you're an employer looking at this knowing nothing else about you.

It can be hard to get separated from your perspective. It's like those times where you're hunting for a bug for hours, and as soon as you get someone else to look for it, she'll see the problem. Stand back from your work as much as you can.

Give a printed copy to a friend, and see what he finds. Give it to your spouse or your parents. The programmer's principle of "Given enough eyes, all bugs are shallow" applies here. The more people who look at your printed output, the more likely someone will catch a mistake.

> Have someone else look at your printed résumé for fresh perspective.

Once you're sure it looks good on paper, test that it looks good printed from other computers besides yours. Email the .doc file to a friend to make sure it looks OK on a computer other than yours. Best of all is if your friend has a different operating system, a different printer, and none of your fonts. Or maybe take it on a thumb drive to Office Max and have them print it there. Try to simulate what will happen when a potential employer prints your résumé.

4.6 Build the HTML Version

The web version of your résumé is as much of a calling card as the Word version, but far more people will see it. Even though you're probably not going to send anyone a copy of this document, it will still be on the Web standing in your place representing you.

Although you want to always tailor a résumé to send to a potential employer, your résumé on the Web will be generic. Since anyone can access it at any time, you won't be customizing it for each potential employer. Fortunately, since it's a web document and you're not as worried about space usage or fitting the résumé to a page or two, you have room to stretch out and don't have to make as many hard decisions such as whether these bullets here are more important than those bullets there.

The first use of your web résumé is as a substitute for your employer-specific résumé. Potential employers are likely to pass around URLs rather than a Word document. Yes, even if the application process requires sending in a Word document. It's easier to pass around a URL rather than a file attachment. The people looking at your web résumé may also not have had any contact with you and are looking for candidates.

Your web résumé also is for employers to find out about you and your skills. You never know when opportunity might come knocking, and having your résumé out on your personal website is an ideal way to keep that door open. This is one reason to make sure your "Buzzwords" section is populated with as many relevant terms and synonyms as you can. It's also why you want to make sure the <title> tag of your web document is as descriptive as possible.

Your web résumé is absolutely not a substitute for following directions when applying for a job. If an ad says to send in a copy of your résumé and you reply with "see my résumé at such-and-such URL," your application letter will win an instant trip to the trash can.

Your online résumé must be easily accessible and usable by anyone in the world. In general, keep things simple. Make sure that it prints nicely. This doesn't mean you need fancy formatting or to make it all fit on a page a certain way, but it does mean that your readers must be able to print it to a printer. Web designers, this means that if you have a Flash version of your portfolio, you still must have a plain old HTML and CSS version of the résumé that a reader can print easily from a browser.

The résumé must also be easily bookmarkable, and the reader must be able to copy and paste the URL from a browser without any hassle. This means your résumé page must not be surrounded by frames and not require an HTTP POST to get to it.

Your résumé's URL should also be as short as possible, just like any URL you'd like people to be able to recall from memory. Put it in a directory of its own so there's no filename or extension to remember. It's better to have http://example.com/resume/ than http://example.com/~steve/personal/resume.jsp.

Construct Your Web Résumé

Don't let Word create your HTML for you.

The first rule of web résumés: do not use "Save As HTML" from Word. Word attempts to replicate the printed look in HTML, instead of creating a web-based document. The HTML that Word generates is filled with Microsoft-specific markup that lets everyone know that you just did a "Save As HTML." Don't do it.

Create the HTML for your web résumé with a good web author-
ing tool, or write it by hand. You're going to look at the final
HTML code anyway, so you may just want to write the HTML
by hand. It's the twenty-first century, and everything is on the
Web. Every techie should know HTML, even if it's not a core job
skill you're looking to use.

Start your document like this:

```
<html>
    <head>
        <title>Resume of Susan Reed: Unix System Administrator and Team
            Lead</title>
    </head>
    <body>
        <h1>Resume of Susan Reed: Unix System Administrator and Team
            Lead</h1>
        <p>
            Susan Reed<br>
            123 Sesame St.<br>
            Lexington, KY  53121<br>
            susan@example.com<br>
            http://example.com/resume/
        </p>

        <h1>Experience</h1>
        <h1>Education</h1>
        <h1>Awards &amp; Honors</h1>
        <h1>Buzzwords</h1>
    </body>
</html>
```

Now you have a general skeleton to start with. Note how the
<title> tag is the ultimate summary of you. It's a one-line ver-
sion of your entire résumé, even smaller than your summary.
It's what will show up in web searches when people try to find
you, or people matching your qualifications. Then, repeat it as
your first <h1>, since the <title> tag doesn't show up on the
page, only in the web browser's title bar. You want it in both
places.

From here, it's like you did your Word doc: use only the logical
markup of tags such as <h1> for headings and <ul> and <li>
for your bulleted lists. Fill in the rest of your sections of text, but
don't worry about how it works yet. The styles will come later.

Since you're writing the web version, you may want to sprinkle
hyperlinks throughout the document, perhaps to projects you've

worked on or smaller employers you've worked for. However, you don't want to detract from your résumé by adding unnecessary links. If you went to Podunk State College and the reader wants to find Podunk's website, they'll be able to find the website easily enough. If you worked for Motorola, trust that the reader knows who that is.

Now that the text is all created and HTML is in place, it's time to do some stylistic formatting with Cascading Style Sheets (CSS). CSS allows you to modify the physical presentation of your logical markup like Word's styles do. Doing stylistic formatting with CSS is the flexible way to do formatting, and it shows that you're aware of how things are done on the Web these days. As with Word and HTML, I'm not going to explain here how to use CSS. Plenty of books and online tutorials can give you the basics.

Make sure that all your CSS is kept in the HTML file itself, inside the <head> tags, rather than in an external .css file. This makes sure that if someone saves a copy of your .html file, they get the CSS with it.

The stylistic rules for your HTML résumé are the same as for the Word document. For example, use a sans serif font for the headings and a serif font for the body text, and use fonts that are likely to be available for the user.

Quality Control on Your Web Résumé

The web résumé is even more likely to come under scrutiny than your Word document, especially if you're applying for a job that's at all web-related, so quality control is crucial.

Your HTML must be absolutely correct. Use a validation tool like HTML Tidy[3] to validate that the HTML is correct. HTML Tidy can also reformat your HTML code so that it's indented and formatted properly, like a carefully prepared HTML document should. You can also use the online W3C HTML validator[4] and the W3C CSS validator.[5]

---

3. http://tidy.sourceforge.net
4. http://validator.w3c.org
5. http://jigsaw.w3.org/css-validator/

Regularly check the links in your résumé to make sure they don't get out-of-date, and that the URLs they refer to are still valid.

4.7 Build the Text Document

You may never need a text-only version of your résumé, but when you do, it's important to get it right. Once you come up with one, keep it handy. You want it to look formatted nicely enough to see organization, but without going too far into the ASCII art world.

You'll use your text résumé in two places: email and online forms. In email, you may be asked to include a text-only version of your résumé with an email. If the ad says "Include résumé (no attachments)," they want it text-only, inline in the email. If you're putting your résumé anywhere online, whether a hiring company's website, a job site like Monster, or a community website like SourceForge, you're going to need a text-only résumé.

Your text résumé will have all the same content as either of the other forms, but the only formatting you'll do will be with horizontal spacing for indents and asterisks as bullets. Don't try to approximate any other formatting, such as underlining with underscore characters. Each line of the résumé will end with a hard return (line feed in Unix, CR/LF in Windows) so that there is no word wrapping when the reader looks at it. You're defining the word wrapping at the time of editing. Your main goal is to make it reasonably likely that it will look OK when the recipient reads it, without getting mangled.

The easiest way to start a text version of your résumé is by running the HTML version through Lynx. Lynx[6] is a freely available text-only web browser that ships with many Unix-like operating systems. Lynx helps here because it can save a copy of a web page, rendered to fit in a specified width of monospaced columns.

---

6. http://lynx.browser.org

It will turn your HTML résumé like this:

```
<h2>Technical Skills</h2>
<p>
Perl
<ul>
<li>Ten years Perl experience</li>
<li>Responsible for more than
    <a href="http://search.cpan.org/~petdance/">twenty
    other modules</a></li>
<li>Regular contributor of patches to the Perl core
</ul>
```

into this, which you can use as the base for your text-only résumé:

```
Technical Skills

   Perl

      * Ten years Perl experience
      * Responsible for more than twenty other modules
      * Regular contributor of patches to the Perl core
```

If you have Lynx installed, call it like this: lynx -dump -nolist -width=70 your-resume.html. The option -dump tells Lynx to save the rendered text, -nolist omits the list of hyperlinks, and -width=70 says to not print wider than 70 characters across. The Lynx default of 80 characters is too wide, because you want to make sure that your text-only résumé doesn't get word-wrapped when you send it in email.

4.8 You're Ready to Move Forward

Now you have the foundation of your tools for telling employers about who you are. Your résumé tells about you in words describing you and your skills and about how you view your work by being a solid, competent work product. Nobody expects to be wowed by the look of a résumé, so you're going for good basic work.

Now it's time to find the jobs that interest you and do some work to get hired.

Chapter 5

Finding Your Job

So far, everything I've discussed has been in your control. It has been about what *you* want and how *you* present *your* background. Now the rest of the world comes in to the picture. Now you must find the job.

Searching for a job can be frustrating as you run up against dead ends or exhaust the list of possibilities that you've found without finding what you want. There can be a feeling of dread when you come to the end of the job listings and you still haven't found what you're looking for. Fortunately, it's usually not as bad as you fear. The sources of jobs are infinite if you spend enough time meeting new people, sending email, contacting friends, and searching the Web.

As you read this chapter, remember that finding the job and applying for the job are closely related. Finding the job is also a process of *finding out about* the job. You're researching what it will take to apply for and interview to do the job. Make sure that you read both this chapter and the next, Chapter 6, *Applying for the Job*, on page 109, before you start the job hunt.

5.1 It's All About the People

Before you start googling for *java jobs Cleveland*, before you start building systems to keep track of search engine hits and RSS feeds of job boards, and so on, stop and remember the most important aspect of finding the job.

Your most important tool in finding a job is relationships with other people. The best way to use that tool is with direct conversation. In all your search activities, prefer to work directly with other people. When working with others, choose a phone conversation over email and a face-to-face discussion over a phone conversation.

For geeks who prefer to work with computers or to have conversations over email or IM, this can be a daunting proposition, but it's one you must make happen, for a number of reasons.

The "hidden job market" accounts for 60 to 80 percent of jobs. These are jobs not advertised to the world. They might be internal transfers in your own company or jobs where the employer doesn't bother running an ad. Job advertising is not cheap, and an employer can save a few thousand dollars in advertising by going with a candidate who someone already knows.

Second, people are more likely to want to help if they talk to you directly. The personal approach gives them a face to understand, a person with whom to empathize. Imagine that you get email from someone at work asking for help with a problem, and compare that with her coming to you to ask you directly. Chances are you're more likely to act on the in-person request.

Third, face-to-face dealings have far more bandwidth than electronic communication. Your essential humanity comes through over the phone more than in text, because the other person can hear you, receiving more information. They can get mood, expression, and nuance in your voice in a way that plain old text doesn't convey. Similarly, the massively larger bandwidth of communicating in person trumps the telephone.

All this increased bandwidth and conversation, without the constraints of having to communicate through our fingers, increases our chance for luck—for serendipity to strike. Free-flowing conversations trigger ideas in our brains that might never happened. "You know, I just realized, I think my colleague Steve was saying something about his brother needing a computer person...." Increase your luck, and you may just find the job.

Chance Favors the Prepared Mind

One evening on a commuter train, my prepared mind and willingness to talk to other people helped me get a job filled.

I was taking the train to my home outside Chicago, and I noticed a woman reading *Webmaster in a Nutshell* (SE99). As the train emptied over the next hour, I realized that she probably lived within a reasonable commute distance from McHenry and might be interested in working for my company. I decided to go talk to her.

I handed her my company business card and said, "Hi, my name is Andy Lester, and I'm guessing from your book that you do web work. Do you know anyone who might be looking for a job out in McHenry County?" As it turns out, she was herself looking for a job. I talked about what the company did, she was interested, and after a few interviews, she came on board.

You may say this story is about plain old dumb luck, and you'd be right. However, we can increase our chances of finding luck by getting out in the world to meet with people. Further, while you see a chance, take it. Even a slim chance is better than a zero chance from doing nothing.

Ask People for Help

If personal contacts are the most important part of your job search, then it makes sense to start with them first in your searching. How do you use this resource?

At no point in your search are you asking anyone "Can you give me a job?" It sounds like you're asking for a handout, for charity, to be given something for nothing. People will find this offensive. Instead, what you're asking for is *a little bit of help with finding a job*. People want to help and share knowledge, but they don't want to give you everything.

Think back to when you've been on a tech mailing list or bulletin board and someone posted a question asking "Can someone give me a shell script that backs up my server to a remote host?" The response is usually swift, unforgiving, and acerbic. Compare with someone saying "I'd like to send the contents of a server to a different host as a low-cost backup, but I'm not sure what's best. Is rsync the way to go, or is there a better solution?" When you show that you're asking for a hand up, not a handout, people are more willing, even eager, to help.

It's also important that you not ask anyone to do anything for you or to give them assignments. There's a big difference between "You said before your uncle Steve was a programmer; could you give me his phone number or address?" which is a simple request for information, and "Could you give your uncle Steve a copy of my résumé?" which is now giving the person an assignment, having him or her act as messenger and intermediary. The latter request often leads to uncomfortable situations, and I always refuse them.

How to Ask for Help

Just about anyone you know can help with your job search. Here's a tiny list:

- Your parents and every relative you know

- Members of technical mailing lists you're on

- Your friends at church

- Your neighbors

- The barista who makes your coffee every morning or the guy who runs that little record store you like

- Your Twitter, Facebook, and LinkedIn contacts

- Readers of your blog

- Former co-workers[1]

---

1. I don't recommend discussing your plans to leave a company with current co-workers, even if you've always commiserated with how much you hate the place. It takes only one loose-lipped colleague to accidentally say, "Yeah, Karen's looking for a job, too" to get you fired.

- The reference librarian at your local public library who you chat with while looking for job-hunting guides

- Someone on the train reading a book or magazine that relates to your area of expertise

Given the varied relationships you have with these people, your conversations with them will be different, but the question you'll ask will always be based on the core of "Can you point me to someone who could help me with my search?" It's a low-pressure question that doesn't ask for much but leaves open the entire range of possibilities for the person to help however he or she may feel comfortable with.

Your conversation doesn't have to be a big deal. You're just asking for a pointer to someone else.

You: *Hey, Rick, I don't think I told you, but Yoyodyne laid me off last week.*

Rick: *Geez, that's gotta suck. I guess it was good I left when I did. What are you doin'?*

You: *I had an idea it was coming, and so I'd been working on keeping my résumé up and checking some job boards. Now it's more serious, of course. I wanted to ask whether you'd heard of any places looking for a good DBA or anyone who could help point me in the right direction. Most of the DBA positions I see posted are for Oracle, and I'd like to stay with SQL Server if I could.*

Rick: *No, I really don't. I know that at my new place we don't even have dedicated DBAs. But I'll keep an eye open for you. Give me your email address again in case I hear anything.*

See how you're just asking for a pointer, no pressure, not asking for Rick to actually do anything for you. You're also showing that you've been doing work yourself and that Rick would be helping you along, not doing the bulk of the work. Whether or not Rick has anything for you today, the exchange has great value, because Rick now knows you're looking.

This simple exchange is all there is to it. You will adjust accordingly when talking to Aunt Edna and not bother **Don't forget Aunt Edna.** with tech details, but the core is the same: "Can you suggest a contact to help me get closer to my goal?"

Have these conversations. Make them part of your life. You will grow more comfortable having them, and you will increase your luck.

5.2 Where the Jobs Are

There's no single source for finding the job you love. Use everything together, from newspapers and job sites to working your personal network to everything in between.

As recently as ten years ago, the classified ads in your local newspaper were the single most important source to look for a job. In fact, even in Chicago with two major newspapers, only the *Tribune* was worth looking in, or maybe a local suburban paper. Monster was just starting to gain traction. Today, the options have exploded in number and focus, and the Internet has increased the human networking possibilities exponentially.

Employers

If you know you want to work at a specific company, or are interested in them, of course you know that's the best place to start. Visit its website and search its Careers, Jobs, or Positions Available page. But don't stop there.

Search the Web for job ads for this company. It's entirely possible that the company's own website doesn't have the most recent information on the website, but a job board like CareerBuilder may. Conversely, it's possible that a position has recently been filled and removed from the company website but is still available on Dice or Monster.

Even if the job seems to have been filled, go ahead and apply for it anyway. See the next chapter, Chapter 6, *Applying for the Job*, on page 109.

Local Resources

If you know you're looking in a given geographic area, the first place to check may not be a search engine but a decidedly old-school source: the local Chamber of Commerce. The Chamber of Commerce is a business network created for a given city or regional area, and member businesses join to promote themselves and make contacts. The chamber's website will have member directories and, in many cases, job listings. Many of the businesses will not be ones that have any potential for you, since everyone from the local florist to the single guy with a driveway resurfacing truck will be a Chamber of Commerce member. However, most companies with more than twenty employees or so have IT needs of some kind or another.

Don't stop with the Chamber of Commerce website, however. Each Chamber of Commerce will have an office staffed by real-live humans whose job it is to help member businesses, and part of that is finding talent. The people working for the local chamber know the area well, know the businesses, and can pass along information that you won't get online. If possible, visit in person or make a phone call.

You: Hi, my name is [your name]. I'm looking for a job here in Waterford. I was wondering if I could have a few minutes of your time?

Carol: Sure, I'd be glad to help out. I'm Carol Danvers, and I'm in charge of business relations. What are you looking for?

You: I have seven years of experience in computers [no need for specifics here] working for advertising firms. I checked out the Chamber website, and so of course I noticed Waterford Marketing. I'll be talking to Dan Fielding, their president, tomorrow.

Carol: Oh, good, Dan's a great guy. I've known him for years. Tell him I said "hi."

You: I'll do that. [And make sure you do!] Are there other companies in the area that I should look at first?

Carol: Let me think...I was at a meeting last month with Warren Worthington. He's the vice president of First Bank of Waterford, and he was telling me about some new computer system they were having some growing pains with. You know who else might be interesting? Anderson Manufacturing out on Highway 47 is in the middle of expanding their factory, so I know they're growing. There might be some possibilities there, too.

You: *These are great, thanks very much. [You are writing these down!] I appreciate your time. Here's my business card, if anything else comes to mind, I'd really appreciate it you'd let know?*

Carol: *Sure, and do you have a copy of your résumé just in case?*

You: *Absolutely. Here are three copies. Thanks again very much for your time.*

Note that you're making everything as easy as possible for your contact. First, you're explaining that you've done your own homework. You know how annoying it is to get tech questions on mailing lists from someone who wants you to do all his work for him? The same goes for other people as well. Here, you're letting the contact know what steps you've taken yourself. Second, you're keeping everything high level. No need to explain that you're experienced in Windows Server 2003 and 2008, looking for a 100-seat shop to admin. All your contact needs to remember is "computer person." Third, what you're asking for extremely simple: pointers to other people. Finally, leaving your business card[2] and copies of your résumé means that passing on your information is simple.

Don't be discouraged if the jobs you see aren't a specific match. Try to get in to see a recruiter. If it's a company you want to get into and you're good, then it may turn into something good. This is especially true for some larger companies such as Google. Google typically lists jobs that they need to have filled, but when you actually apply and interview, they may decide that they like you better for a different position. This can be good or bad, depending on whether it fits your goals. Just don't be surprised if it happens to you. Don't be afraid to ask a recruiter or manager for clarification in their goals.

Job Boards

To the techie looking for a job, job boards like Monster and Dice can seem ideal. It's all online, where we're most comfortable, and the jobs are searchable with database selection fields. The attraction of setting a few filters and narrowing down the field to

---

2. Don't use a business card from your current employer. Get your own made at a local print shop for ten bucks.

give you a few jobs that fit your interests and criteria is appealing, almost like ordering from the drive-thru at McDonald's.

You: *Uh, yeah, I'd like to get a Java programming job, I'm in the Cincinnati area, I need to make $75,000, and I have seven years of experience.*

Job Board: *Did you want a hot apple pie with that?*

You: *No, but I do want a company with fewer than 100 employees.*

Job Board: *Thank you, please pull around for your six search results and to upload your résumé in a plain-text format that will mangle your formatting.*

It may be as easy as ordering at McDonald's, but the chances aren't good you'll get a gourmet-quality job.

This kind of approach is great for buying things online. If you want to buy a new printer that prints ten pages per minute, prints double-sided, and is within a certain price range, it's a great way to do it. You get your two or three choices and then choose from the few.

The problem is twofold: you're not an interchangeable product, and neither is the job.

Job boards reduce the job-hunting process to moving around interchangeable people into interchangeable jobs. For many companies that have hundreds of similar positions to fill, this is how they have to do it. They put out generic job descriptions and comb through applicants searching for you like you're that 10 PPM double-sided printer for less than $400.

Posting a résumé on one of the megaboards will certainly get you attention if you have decent qualifications, but it may be more attention than you're looking for. Recruiters who see you as a number will email or call you, trying to fit you into a position for which you may have no interest.

Never forget that the big job boards aren't there to help you get a job. They exist to sell ad space. CareerBuilder, one of the largest job boards, states it proudly in its mission statement:

> "Our mission is to be the global leader in online recruitment advertising by being an employee-driven,

customer-focused organization that provides the best rate of return to our stakeholders."[3]

Commercial job boards are there to sell ads, not help you.	There's nothing in there about you and your job. CareerBuilder is focused on "online recruitment advertising." It's there to put job ads in front of your face.

The Hard Numbers on Job Boards

So, you may think, "Fine, the job boards sell ads, but aren't they good at getting people jobs?" The numbers don't seem to say so.

As part of their yearly Source of Hire study,[4] in early 2008 Gerry Crispin and Mark Mehler collected data from fifty-nine large high-profile companies describing the sources of their hires. The numbers don't look good for the job boards.

Source of Hire	External Hires from This Source
Niche job boards	0.7%
http://hotjobs.com	1.0%
http://careerbuilder.com	4.5%
http://monster.com	5.0%
Company website	14.0%
Referrals from people	28.7%

Job boards should not be your primary focus.	These statistics may not matter to the question of whether CareerBuilder is fulfilling its mission of being the "leader in online recruiting advertising," but

they don't speak well of its value to you, the job hunter. The top three job boards combined don't deliver hires to companies as well as the company's own website, and referrals still dwarf all four of those sources.

Similar statistics gathered for only the tech industry or with smaller firms might give slightly different numbers, but I suspect they won't be that much different. The conclusion seems clear: job boards can be part of your job search but should not be the primary focus.

---

3. http://www.careerbuilder.com/share/AboutUs/, January 3, 2009
4. http://www.careerxroads.com/news/SourcesOfHire08.pdf

Even if they don't deliver candidates, Monster and the like can still be valuable to the job hunter. If nothing else, they are excellent research tools for getting a sense of the job market and what employers are looking for, especially in a given geographic area. When researching your next move, this sort of data aggregation and drill-down is ideal. It's a case where you *do* want to look at the jobs available as an impersonal aggregate.

One of the problems with the database-driven approach to collecting job candidates is that each job has to fit into a well-defined bucket, and jobs rarely do. For example, when I go to http://job.com, I'm asked what state I want to search. Where I live in northern Illinois, a job in Milwaukee, Wisconsin, is no farther than a job in Chicago, Illinois, but I don't get to choose multiple states. The job categorization is worse. I've spent the last seven years working as a computer programmer and manager for an e-commerce website. The site offers me a drop-down labeled "Job Category." Which of these do I choose?

- E-commerce

- Information Tech/Computer

- Internet/Web

- Management

Any of the four categories would be appropriate, so I have a 25 percent chance of hitting the one that someone looking for my skillset will check.

Still, job boards can be an important part of your job search. The following are some of the different types of boards you can use. I don't discuss features of any individual boards, because chances are that as soon as this book is printed,[5] the site will change. It's best that you try some out and see which you feel most comfortable with.

Don't worry too much that you're missing something on the board you're skipping. These competing boards have lots of overlap, at least with the biggies like Monster and Dice.

---

5. Or as soon as the gerbils at the Pragmatic Bookstore finish hand-crafting the PDF with their teeny-tiny gerbil hands.

- General job boards: http://monster.com, http://careerbuilder.com, and so on

  For a while, Monster was the canonical job board. Monster and now CareerBuilder cover the entire range of employment, meaning you can search for a job as a janitor in addition to a programmer if you want. However, if you're looking for a job far from your current location, that may be a place to check.

- Techie-specific: http://dice.com, http://computerjobs.com, and so on

  Dice is the current king of tech job boards, but there are plenty of others like http://computerjobs.com that are worth checking out. One nice part of computerjobs.com is its use of DNS, so http://linux.computerjobs.com automatically gives you Linux jobs.

- Technology-specific: http://jobs.perl.org, http://jobs.rubyinside.com, and so on

  Job boards tied to a specific technology, whether Windows sysadmins or Perl programmers, often have the advantage of doing the job search focusing for you, by virtue of their clientele. They also often have the advantage of being maintained by fans and devotees of the technology, so the quality of candidates ought to be higher. If you know that you're looking for a job focused on a specific language, start with boards like these.

- Local general boards: http://craigslist.com, your local newspaper's website

  Craigslist and your local newspaper have the advantage of narrowing your search geographically without having the vagaries of the "within N miles of your ZIP code" job listings that most job boards have. Craigslist also happens to be free for employers to post their jobs, so it may be the first place that an employer will post. A check of Craigslist should always be a regular part of your job search.

- Industry-specific boards

  If you want to focus your search on a specific industry, there are plenty of boards out there that target that.

For instance, if I wanted to work in the insurance industry, http://insurancejobs.com currently shows three IT jobs in Illinois. Dikel & Roehm's *Guide to Internet Job Searching* [DR08], updated yearly, lists hundreds of websites like these.

- Aggregators: http://simplyhired.com, http://juju.com, and so on

Aggregators like SimplyHired gather jobs from the job boards all over and allow you to search them at one go. The idea is that you'll find the job you want in a single place, rather than having to visit all the job boards that the aggregator scrapes. In a search for Perl jobs in Chicago, the first page of results at SimplyHired gave me jobs from Dice, Net-Temps, jobs.perl.org, ComputerJobs.com, and HotJobs.

The prospect of searching through dozens of job boards at once may seem simple, but you're still having to sift through job ads that may or may not apply to you. It may turn out to be simply growing the size of the haystack in which to find the needle.

Newspapers

Newspaper classifieds are still worth checking. Don't fall into the trap of thinking that a forward-thinking, technologically-savvy company wouldn't bother with print advertising. However, newspaper ads should should not be your first choice.

Print ads can also be troublesome because of overlap with websites. Most newspapers publish their print ads on their websites, but this is not always the case. It may be an option that the listing employer chooses not to use. You'll need to be careful tracking the jobs you respond to in order to avoid responding to the same ad twice from two different sources.

One big advantage of newspaper ads is to get a high-level visual view of what's available in your area. Say you're looking to do Perl or PHP work and it feels like the available positions advertised are outside of these areas. You *could* do some Java, but you'd rather not. All Windows- or mainframe-based jobs are definitely a big "no."

Don't Job Hunt on Company Time

Never conduct your job search on company time or using any company resources. Never mind the ethical issues of getting paid by your current company to find work at another, it's also a great way to lose your current job a lot sooner than you wanted. It's especially tacky to use your company email account for any correspondence.

Here's an exercise to try. Go through the ads in the Sunday paper of your nearest big city, and mark each ad according to your level of interest. For each Perl or PHP ad, mark it with a green letter "P" if it's something you'd be interested or qualified for, and use a red "P" if you're uninterested. For the Java positions, mark a big red "J." If it's a job that sounds interesting, but for which you don't have the skills, mark a purple "U." All the other ads, leave unmarked.

At the end of the process, you have a low-tech but quantitative view of the jobs advertised in your area. Where you see green, you see potential jobs that you'd be happy with. Red shows where you could get by if you had to but would rather not. Purple means a job you could take if you had better or different skills. No color means there's no possibility there for you.

Now, take a look at the grid of colors in your mini art project. What do you see most? If you have many red "J"s or "P"s, ask yourself whether you're being too picky in what you select. If you're awash in purple "U"s, you could probably stand to broaden your horizons. If very little of the paper is marked at all, it's probably a combination of both.

With so many sources of job leads, your job leads are multiplied, but this also means you'll need to be careful to not follow up on leads twice. There is no single source of all job listings, even the job listing aggregators. Your hunting will necessarily include seeing many of the same jobs over and over. Keep careful notes on the jobs you find to ensure that you don't follow up on the same job twice. See Section 5.6, *Work the Hunt*, on page 105 for more on doing this right.

Always be passively checking these sources of job leads, even if you're perfectly happy at your current job. Set up an RSS feed in your newsreader for

> Always be looking for your next great job.

jobs matching your interests, or sign up for email alerts for appropriate jobs. CareerBuilder has a good email alert system that sends out recent job listings, sorted by distance from my home ZIP code. It's trivial for me to scan the listings in my inbox every few days.

There is no sin in keeping an eye open for better possibilities. It keeps you looking out for what could be better and lets you be confident that your current position is the best there is.

Read Section 12.4, *Always Look for Your Next Job*, on page 230 for more.

5.3 What to Find Out About a Potential Job

When you've found a job that looks like it's interesting, the search is only half over. Now the research phase begins.

Don't even think about pursuing a job lead without researching as much as you can about the company. You have two big questions to answer about the company:

- Does it seem likely that I would want to work for this company?

- How does the company make money, and how do I help it make more money? Corrolary: what questions do I need to ask before the interview to find out the answer so I am prepared?

Are You Likely to Want This Job?

The first question is to determine whether it's worth pursuing the company at all. If you don't think it's likely you'll want to take the job, then don't waste your time and patience. Unless you have very low standards, there aren't 100 jobs out there that will fit your needs, so you must focus only on the ones that matter. It's better to spend serious amounts of time on a job where you're great for each other than three or four that are only so-so. A few hours of research up front is far better than wasting days of preparation and interview or, worse, actually taking a job that's a good fit for you that you wind up leaving in a month or two.

How Does the Company Make Money, and How Can You Help Make More Money?

If you decide you want the job, move on to these questions: What does the company make? What services does it provide? Who are its customers? How has business been? Who are its competitors? How is it using technology? Is your position using new technology? Is the technology new to the company?

This part of the research requires you to wear your "Think like the hiring manager" hat firmly atop your head.

5.4 Do Your Detective Work

No job ad or lead from a friend is going to include all the information to answer all your questions. You're going to have to do some work on your own.

This detective work can be time-consuming, but it's a fantastic investment. If your research turns up a nugget of information that lets you tailor the interview exactly to the needs of the company and you land the job because of it, that's a huge payoff. If, on the other hand, you discover something horrifying that saves you from pursuing a job that would have had you running screaming after two weeks, that's an even bigger payoff.

> Never pursue a job without researching the company.

Many interviewers, including me, will ask about how the candidate has prepared for the interview. It could be implicit like "So, what do you know about Yoyodyne?" or it can be explicit as in "Tell me what you did to prepare for this interview, including any research you did and what you found." You'll look like a chump if your answer comes down to "Uh, I just kinda showed up today." Even if you're not asked about your research, research is excellent anti-chump protection.

The company will research you before calling you in for an interview or even a phone screen. You owe it to yourself to do the same research on the company. The company calls it "due diligence," and you should, too.

The Company Itself

The place to start is also the most obvious. Read the company's website, with an eye to answering your two big questions.

Read every page you can with titles like these:

- Contact
- About Us
- For Investors
- Media Relations
- Jobs

These pages show how the company wants to present itself to the outside world. They are your first indication of what the company finds important. Use these pages to answer these questions for yourself:

- What does the company create or sell? What services does it provide?
- Who are the company's customers? Does it sell to consumers or other businesses?
- How big an operation is it? Regional, national, multinational? Is it part of a larger corporate parent?
- How long has the company been in business? What changes has it gone through over time?
- If it's a publicly traded company, look at its annual reports. How has it fared over the past five years? Why?

Take these questions seriously, and don't just gloss over the answers. You should be talking about them in the interview. Anyone can walk in having glanced at the website and think "I guess these guys sell farm stuff." It's quite another to be able to talk to your interviewer about how the company sells feed systems to cattle farms mostly in the southwest United States, although business has been off in the past year because of a drought. It also opens up other questions for further research.

There are also plenty of questions to think about that relate to your decision as to whether this company would be one you'd like to work for.

For example:

- Is the company's business interesting to you? Why or why not?

- What does the company show off most? Where is the company's pride? If the site talks about valuing people, is it using stock photos or real customers and real employees?

- Are you likely to know any of its customers or anyone in its target market you could talk to? Maybe your Uncle Steve in Albuquerque knows some cattle farmers who have opinions about your prospective employer.

Ask critical questions as well. Why is the company hiring so many programmers? Has there been a lot of turnover lately? That'd be a good thing to ask. Why is the company advertising for three vice president positions at once? Is there upheaval in the higher ranks? Again, that may be a good question to ask to get a sense of the stability of the company.

Finally, you may also get information from the public relations department of the company, if it's large enough. Although typically geared toward media requests, the PR department can handle questions about the company's operations, and so on, but don't expect to find too much more than is available publicly online.

Your Contacts

Revisit the list of people you talked to when you first started looking, discussed in Section 5.1, *How to Ask for Help*, on page 82. Go back to those people and see whether anyone has the scoop on the job or company you're looking at. As with asking for help, you're just going to ask a few low-key questions that are openers for information about the company. You might drop an email to your friend Doug and say, "Hey, Doug, I'm looking into a job over at Yoyodyne and wanted to get some insight to what it's like over there. Do you know anyone who works there?"

That same request can be forwarded to mailing lists that might be relevant. If you're on a local techie mailing list, say, for the Poughkeepsie PostgreSQL Users Group, post a brief note to the list.

I'm looking around for jobs, and I've seen an interesting
position available at Yoyodyne (include URL). The ad says
that it would include some PostgreSQL administration. Has
anyone here worked for Yoyodyne and would be willing to
answer a few questions about it? These are some basic questions:

* What did you work on while you were there?
* Did you like it?
* What can they improve in?
* Would you recommend them as an employer?

Of course, if you'd rather not reply in public, please
email me directly at andy@theworkinggeek.com, and I'll
keep the comments confidential.

Thanks for any help you can provide.

As with any other request for help, keep the requests simple
and not overwhelming, and provide other options to encourage
people to respond.

Not-Quite-Random Web Searching

Once you've read the company website and you've gotten the
official line about what the company is and does, now it's time
for the real web detective work for information about the company on the Web that it can't control. You're going to search for
references to the company, both by name and by references to
its website.

Start with a Google search for the
company name itself: *example.com.* If
you find an email address, search for
that and see what the person might
have to say on sites other than the
parent site: *bob.smith@example.com -*

> Communications from
> employees speak
> volumes about a
> company.

site:example.com. This will search for the email address, but
exclude hits on *example.com* itself. Also look for sites that
link to the company's site, and see what they have to say:
link:example.com.

Check Google Groups[6] and other mailing list archives. If you can turn the email address of someone who works in a technical area at the company and then search for his or her postings to technical mailing lists, you can get quite an impression of what things are like.

```
To: mysql-help@...
From: bsmith@example.com
Subject: Help w/mysql URGENT
Date: (a few months ago)

Hey can anyone help with mysql perms. I am dba for my company
and we have a mysql install and i think i f\$\#*!ed something
when i installed a patch lol!

i am trying to go 2 the company dir. page on the intranet and i
keep getting some kind of permison errors. what should i do?
```

This example is cartoonishly bad, but not at all implausible. The author of that email does not give a good impression about himself or the company he works for, since them employ him. However, don't discount a company because of one bad email or one bad employee. It's one view of the company, and, who knows, maybe the job advertised would include replacing that guy. Then again, a company that hires people like that may have problems endemic throughout the organization.

If the company has multiple domain names and presences, check those as well. Grain Delivery Co. might be graindelivery-inc.com on its main website but might also have a separate website at graintoday.com that is more customer-facing, perhaps a customer portal. Check for links to and email addresses from that domain as well.

Check alternate spellings and misspellings. I work for Follett Corporation, but plenty of people online spell it "Follet," with only one *T*, and many people call it "Follett's." I'd be searching on both those variants if I were researching a job here. Of course, don't stick to Google. Even though it's the most popular search engine, others like MSN Live Search will probably have pages that Google does not.

---

6. http://groups.google.com

Here are some questions you won't get the answer to on the company website but may well discover with some vigorous work on Google:

- Have there been layoffs recently? How often do they happen? At some companies the layoffs are a quarterly fear festival.
- What's it like to work there?
- Do employees from the company seem unhappy?
- How has technology changed over time?

Check Out Their Operations

If the company has any presence available to the public, check it out. If they're a retail operation, visit one of their stores. Is the store dirty? Do they do things on the cheap? If a company is going to go cheap on its customer-facing aspects, it's not likely they'll be spending the dollars necessary to get you a fast desktop machine or the server power you need.

Chat up one of the employees about how he or she likes it there. Sure, a back-office sysadmin job is very different from someone working in front-line retail, but surly attitudes and disaffection are often endemic throughout an entire company.

Call the customer support line or a sales phone number with some questions about the products that they sell. Does the person seem knowledgeable? Happy? Is the person someone you would enjoy working with? You very well may be if you work for that company.

As with any other research you do, nothing you find should necessarily be a deal-breaker, making you turn away from the company as a potential employer. However, consider the trends that you see, and add questions to your list to ask at an interview. You might ask something like "I stopped by the storefront on Elm and heard a clerk griping about the cash register being old and always broken. Do you run into that sort of situation in IT as well?"

Current and Former Employees

Probably the most valuable source of information about an employer is from someone who has worked there. If you know someone who works at the company, then you've got it made. You can ask all your tough questions. But what if you don't know anyone there? How do you find them?

Some applied web searching will probably turn up some employees. Once you find someone you know works there, you've got a thread to hold on to. Maybe you'll find the person's blog, where he gripes about some dumb new policy at work. You might find a mailing list thread that gives insight into what operations are like there.

When you do find an employee, keep track of this crucial lead. Track URLs that you've found so that you can refer to them later if necessary. Chances are you'll want to do further research without wasting time re-googling the same pages. This is especially true if you're researching a company that you'd like to work at but that doesn't currently have any openings.

Finding a home email address is the best of all. Go ahead and send a polite email to the person asking for their impressions of the company and working there. Also include a request for help as discussed in Section 5.1, *Ask People for Help*, on page 81. Here's an example:

```
Subject: Looking for advice about working at Yoyodyne

Hi, Bob,

My name is Andy Lester, and I'm considering applying for a
programming position at Yoyodyne (include URL for the ad).
I see from your post to the Solaris Administrators Forum
(include URL) that you work there, or did in the past. From
your posts on the forum, you seem like you'd be willing to help
with some questions I had about Yoyodyne. I'd like to ask for
any advice or insight that might help me in my search.

What can you tell me about your time there? Do you like working
there? What didn't you like?  What sorts of projects were you
working on? Most of all, would you recommend them as a place
to work?

If there's someone else who might be a better person to ask, can
you please point me to him or her? Also, if you'd rather not
discuss this in email, I can be reached at 815-555-1212.

Thank you very much for any assistance you can provide.
```

Notice a few things from this sample. First, never send an email like this to someone's work account. Many employers monitor employee email. Make sure that your email doesn't look or sound like automated spam, or it may get deleted unread. A subject like "Advice" from an unknown mail account may well make the recipient think it's spam.

Make sure that the recipient doesn't *feel* like he's been spammed. Make it clear that you're not just shotgunning this request to everyone you can. Also make clear that this email is business-only, too, especially if you're mailing someone of the opposite sex.

Pick a handful of open-ended questions that are most important to you. Don't overwhelm the person with questions, or you lower his likelihood of replying to you. However, always end with the most important question: "Would you recommend it as a good place to work?"

Provide the recipient an alternative to mailing you back, too. Note how the example lists a phone number and a request for another person's name. This gives the person a way to help that might feel less awkward.

If the person writes back, thank him or her for their time, no matter what it is that they say. Even if you get back a "I'd rather not discuss Yoyodyne because...," you still write back and say, "I understand completely, and I thank you for your time and wish you good luck in the future."

Blind-mailing an employee or former employee is high-risk, high-reward. You may well get back nothing, but if you do, the payoff is fantastic.

Social Websites

The explosion of social websites like MySpace and Facebook has spawned business-oriented websites, too. The biggest, LinkedIn, is an ideal source for finding people who work at, or have worked at, your company of interest.

LinkedIn isn't just a big index of email addresses so you can mail your questions to people, but it's a start. There are rules about how you can contact other LinkedIn members based on how many degrees of separation away from you they are, but at the very least you can usually get names for further detective work. LinkedIn profiles also include endorsements from others. These can also give you insight into the processes about the job you're looking at.

If you can find the hiring manager for the position you're looking at in LinkedIn, you've hit pay dirt. Find out about his or her past history. Is she new to management? What did she do before the current job? What do her people think of her?

Even without contacting the people involved, LinkedIn can be a great source of information, as Pete found:

The Value of Turning Over Some Rocks
by Pete Krawczyk, Developer, Wonder Lake, Illinois

A friend of mine, "John," got a call from a headhunter to interview with another company, "Acme Widgets," for a similar position. After the phone screen, John asked my opinion about the company.

I hadn't heard of Acme Widgets before, so I did a simple Google search. After that, I did a LinkedIn search to see whether I knew anyone from Acme. Even though I didn't, I saw one of the "co-founders" had been working there for 16 months. When I mentioned this to John, he was surprised. "I've been told longer, like since around 2000."

I showed John what I found and how I found it. Further research showed several people who worked at Acme less than a year, suggesting a high turnover rate. After our research, John decided to go ahead with the phone interview, but now he was armed with better questions about the company. "I was told they were incorporated earlier," John said, "but that was the headhunter, and I found him to be like a used-car salesman."

Other social websites are worth investigating as well but are less business-oriented. Poke around Facebook for a while, and you may find as many contacts as on the websites aimed at the business networking user base. Of course, by the time you read this, there may be other social networking sites that have popped up to peruse.

5.5 Headhunters

Conventional wisdom makes the idea of working with a head-hunter an appealing one. You visit the headhunter, you hand over a copy of your latest résumé in Word format, and the headhunter flips through his file of job openings, looking for the one that's just right for you. "Ah, here we go," he beams, "an easy 9-to-5 job paying an absurdly high salary, but they've been waiting for someone with exactly your skills!" Boy, that was easy.

If only it were so.

To get the expert view on headhunters, I spoke with Nick Corcodilos, host of http://asktheheadhunter.com and author of *Ask the Headhunter* [Cor97]. He told me that the misconception that most people have is that headhunters find jobs for candidates. That's backwards. Headhunters are paid by employers to find people to fill specific positions.

This certainly didn't match up with my understanding of how headhunters worked. They usually seemed like commodity brokers, trying to shuffle job candidates through the system however they can. I get an average of two or three cold calls on my work phone, and at least a dozen emails, from headhunters every month. If I talk to one, I can hear he's in a big bullpen, a room full of other headhunters, all working the phones. He asks whether I'm looking for any new opportunities, can I send him an updated copy of my résumé in Word format, and do I know anyone else who might be looking for a new job? These guys are playing the numbers, the same mathematical formula that keeps spammers in business, because it doesn't matter how many people you bother if you get that one hit.

Corcodilos explained that these guys are from employment agencies and are not what he calls headhunters. They play both sides of the hunt, for both employer and candidate, circulating résumés of people who come in looking for a job. They're working the process by numbers, trying to get as many résumés in front of as many hiring authorities as possible. In short, they're not doing anything more than you could do yourself.

Headhunters typically are paid a significant percentage of the position's salary + bonus, from 15 to 25 percent. For an $80,000/year programmer, that can be up to $20,000. At those

---

Never Pay to Find a Job

Headhunters, employment agencies, and the like are hired by and paid by the companies with the jobs. A legitimate agency will never ask you to pay a fee for distribution of your résumé or contacting a company. If you're ever asked for money of any kind from a head-hunter, walk away immediately.

---

kinds of fees, I'd have thought that it would only be high-level positions that get headhunted, but Nick says it could be anyone from a mid-level programmer all the way up to VP-level position.

So if it's a matter of being sought by headhunters, what should you do to be noticed? Corcodilos says that you need to be some-one known in your industry, someone that people know as an expert, a top-level performer that will justify the price that the headhunter is charging for bringing you to the attention of his client firm.

None of this is to say that headhunters have no value to you. A headhunter who knows you and knows your qualifications is a headhunter who can turn to you when faced with a job that matches up with you. There can be value in having a relation-ship with a headhunter. The trouble can be figuring out who to work with.

There's one headhunter I've worked with over the last decade, ˙ and he emails me every year or so to see how things are going. We exchange some email where I tell about what I've worked on recently, and he talks about the state of the job market as he sees it and what the trends are. It's strictly informative, and he's not trying to sell me on any gig. Similarly, if I know anyone looking for jobs in the industries he specializes in, I'll send them his way.

I don't expect anything from him, nor he from me, but we both know each other well and know that if there's a match for what we need, we can turn to the other. It's like buying a lottery ticket. It doesn't cost a lot, and it might just pay off. Just don't rely on it.

5.6 Work the Hunt

Now it's time to get to hunting and search for the job that suits you. As a techie, you have a better-than-average understanding of the Internet and of tracking data, so use it to your advantage. You can use the tools or create your own,[7] better than the average person, so do it. You're going to use the Web for research, but you also need to track your search.

You need to track every aspect of your job search, including both actions you've taken and what you've learned. As you search for companies worth your time and make contacts with the people therein, log what you do in exacting detail. It's important that you know what you've said to people and discovered about the company so that you don't embarrass yourself by seeming that you don't know what you're doing. Imagine this phone conversation where you're called at home by the hiring manager who wants to do a phone screen:

Hiring manager: Hello, is this Bob Smith? I'm Doug Jones from Yoyodyne, and I've calling about the job you applied for. I'd just like to ask you a few questions if you have some time.

You: Sure, that's fine. Now, Yoyodyne, you're that web advertising company down in Greenville, right?

Hiring manager: Mmmm, no, we're a plumbing supply distributor in Lakemoor.

You: Oh, right! You're the place that...I think it's my brother-in-law, Dave, works there, probably in accounting.

Hiring manager: Hmmm, I know everybody in accounting, and there hasn't been any Dave that I know of. So, I had a few questions. First, I'm interested in your background using Visual Basic.

You: Oh, what résumé do you have? I think you might have an old one. I mean, I know Visual Basic, but it's not really a strong point. Lately I've been doing more with Oracle. Does the résumé you have say...?

---

7. If you create a tracking system of some kind, you've got something for your portfolio. See Section 7.4, *Prepare a Relevant Portfolio*, on page 125.

This conversation takes place over the phone, but it just as easily could have been at the interview. It shows you as the candidate to be ill-prepared and unorganized. How do you avoid this?

Keep meticulous notes, and keep them ready for easy access. How you keep them is up to you, but they need to be easy to refer to. Start by keeping notes about every aspect of the company. If you find interesting information on the Web, for example, copy & paste it into your notes and keep the URL. Keep all copies of documents that you send out, including emails, résumés, anything. Since you're not going to be sending out canned résumés and canned application letters (Chapter 6, *Applying for the Job*, on page 109), you'll need to know what you sent to each company, and you're just not going to be able to keep it all in your head, especially if you're nervous. Keeping detailed notes lets you print them out and bring them to the interview, too. Take a look at how that embarrassing phone call would have gone with careful note taking.

Hiring manager: *Hello, is this Bob Smith? I'm Doug Jones from Yoyodyne.*

You: *Oh, yes, thanks for calling. I'd love to talk, but right this second isn't great. Can I please call you back in five minutes?*

Of course, Doug says that you can call back in five minutes. You grab your notes, open your saved Word documents, and call him back in exactly five minutes.

You: *Thanks again for calling, Mr. Jones. How are things in the plumbing supply business? My sister-in-law, Amy Egan in marketing, says she's being kept pretty busy.*

Hiring manager: *You're related to Amy? She seems like a great addition to that department, although we don't talk much. Mostly I've been working on migration to Oracle Forms, and that's what I wanted to talk to you about.*

You: *Yes, it was one of the things that stood out in your ad in the Northwest Herald, that you were looking for expertise in Oracle Forms. If you have a copy of my résumé there, you'll see that I've spent the last two years in a situation that sounds much like yours....*

This conversation went well, but it was all because of the preparation and note taking that led up to it. Consider all the facts that you were able to recall from your notes:

- What the company does

- Who you know at the company

- How you found out about the job

- What interested you in the job

- The exact résumé and cover letter that the person at the other end of the phone is looking at

As you track the jobs you're interested in, be aware of dupes. So many of the jobs listed online are reposts of other jobs that it's easy to get confused on what's what. You don't want to apply for the same job twice by mistake. If you find a job you're tracking in a second online source, just make a note of it. Make sure you keep track of the full URL for the job, not just "Found it on CareerBuilder."

You'll also keep track of all interactions with anyone about the job or the company. If you talk to someone at the company, such as doing research on it before applying, log it. If you send a résumé and cover letter, log it and keep a copy of the exact documents you sent. If you talk to someone about the company, even if she doesn't work there, log it. It's much better to be able to say at an interview "I'd spoken to Kristen Henderson over at Yoyodyne about how she'd heard about your Linux upgrade project" than to be mumble-mouthed and saying "Oh yeah, I talked to...oh, what was her name, she was talking about some Linux thing you did that was cool...."

This kind of tracking may seem tedious at the time, but the payoff will make it worthwhile.

5.7 Summary

The searching process may be the longest, and most dispiriting, part of getting a new job, but don't let it get you down. Turn the process into a project like any work-related project. Track your progress and measure your results so you can see how things are going.

Most of all, don't rely on others such as employment agencies or job boards to find your job for you. Blind luck may well favor you with a fantastic opportunity, but you have to help yourself along the way.

Chapter 6

Applying for the Job

Applying for the job is often your first contact with the company. You're going from outside observer to active participant in the process. How you apply, what you send, and every interaction you have with every person along the way is evidence showing those you hope to work for what kind of work you do and what you'll be like to work with. Make it your best.

This process cannot be done by rote, where you send out Yet Another Résumé to Yet Another Company. First, mass-mailed résumés have a stink about them that hiring managers can smell. The odor of mass-produced generic blather is a turnoff for anyone who wants to get an enthusiastic employee who will fit with the team. Second, putting your personality and specifics about how you view a given opportunity forces you to consider carefully whether this job is one for you. If you can't come up with two paragraphs in a cover letter that explains why you are a good match for this job at this company, then you probably shouldn't be applying.

Applying for a job is not a game of numbers. Spraying your résumé across the Internet in the hopes of getting a nibble just doesn't work, because for every

There aren't 100 jobs that are a good fit.

job you send off a bland, uninteresting cover letter to, there are 100 other dopes doing the same thing.

Don't apply for every job you see that might fit. Instead, focus on the ones that matter, and put everything you can into them.

6.1 Customize Your Résumé

You have a great basic résumé, but that's only the first step. Now you customize it.

The résumé is the workhorse of your application package. As I emphasized back in Chapter 3, *Résumé Content: Getting the Words Down*, on page 35, every résumé you send must be created with the specifics of the company and position for which you're applying. Bring out the parts of your background that will help the hiring manager most.

Take a copy of your stock résumé and see it through the eyes of the hiring manager for the job for which you're applying. Think about what on your résumé will be most important to the manager and to the company and how they can use you in their business. You're going to take these words and make them bold to draw attention to them in the initial scanning of your résumé, as explained in Section 4.4, *Create an Effective Summary*, on page 70.

Start by checking the job requirements. Say you have a job ad looking for ASP.NET and SQL Server experience, so those are your first two callout words. In the "Summary" section of your résumé, make those two strings, "ASP.NET" and "SQL Server," and only those two strings, bold. Chances are they're already bolded if you're starting with a stock résumé.

Find other words and concepts in your résumé that correspond to what the company is looking for. You'll probably have words and phrases to emphasize that are not explicitly stated in the ad. If they're looking for a senior project manager, then highlight your many years of experience. If the company is in the financial industry, then drawing attention to jobs you've had in the financial or related industries is appropriate.

This is where researching the company before applying pays off. If you find out, say, that the company takes on mostly government contracts and you have experience in that area in your past, then bold it in your résumé. You'll have an edge over other applicants.

Be judicious in how much bolding you do. Making too many words bold diminishes the effectiveness, like high- lighting entire paragraphs of textbooks

Highlight key words, but don't overwhelm.

instead of key words or sentences. You want the reader's eye drawn to the bold words as the most important ones on the page.

Anywhere you've quantified your value in the résumé, such as in bullets for a given position, you have an excellent candidate for bolding. Don't bold the entire bullet, just the juiciest part. The reader will read the rest for the context. Phrases like these are great to call attention to:

- Introduced test-driven development that **reduced defects by 27%** per KLOC
- **Saved $19,200** in two years by converting servers to Linux
- Redesigned website led to **43% more traffic** and **18% higher clickthrough** in the first six months

As you select these items to highlight, make sure that you can discuss them in an interview or a phone screen, because they'll likely be top questions for the interviewer. "You say you saved $19,200 by converting to Linux. Is that just licensing costs or total cost of ownership? How did you measure those costs?" Maybe it was your boss who came up with that figure to trumpet in the company newsletter, but you'd better to be able to discuss it more intelligently than "I dunno, that's what my boss said."

Don't be afraid to add or remove content from your résumé. Build up the jobs that most closely relate to the position or that help you best tell the story of how you'll help the company and whittle away at the jobs that don't. There's no rule that all sec- tions of your résumé must contain equal numbers of bullets or the same amount of space on the page.

However you juggle the words, you should probably have two to four words or phrases in your summary that are bold because they directly relate to the job. If not, there's a disconnect. Either you're not qualified for this job because the important parts of the job aren't worthy of placing in your summary, or you haven't organized the résumé well. Modify the résumé, or reconsider the job.

6.2 Create a Cover Letter

Rule #1 for cover letters: "Write one." Many people ask, "Do I have to send a cover letter if they don't ask for one?" I can only answer with, "Only if you want a better chance of getting the job."

The cover letter introduces yourself to the reader and tells her things that might not be on the résumé or highlights those that are. A cover letter is personalized. That's not to say that you shouldn't personalize the résumé, but the cover letter is more conversational and allows you to stretch out some more than a résumé.

The reader of your cover letter should be convinced that you are interested in the job. The hiring manager reads more than enough form letters all day from mass-mailers who are just looking for any old job.

Your job in a cover letter is to introduce yourself to the hiring manager and give some context for you and your résumé. The cover letter should do the following:

- Explain where you found out about the job
- Explain what you bring to the company and how it fits with what you're looking for
- Show that you have researched the company
- Tell about any contacts with people you may have at the company
- Show that you care enough about this job to send a personal letter and show that you want not just *any*, but *this* job

 Here's how not to do a cover letter, an example I received while looking for a programmer:

```
Dear Prospective Employer,

Your Advertisement on jobs.perl.com for a

    Sr. Prog. for library book wholesaler

caught my attention. I would like to apply. I am confident that
I can perform the job effectively. My background and career
goal, seem to match the job requirements well.
```

This letter tells plenty about the author, none of it good:

- He's indiscriminate, throwing his résumé out to anyone where he finds an ad. He's probably desperate.
- He's careless. "Sr. Prog. for library book wholesaler" was the title of the job posting, not the name of the position. The actual website was jobs.perl.org, not jobs.perl.com. Plus, there are errors in English mechanics.
- He doesn't care about the quality of his work sending out such an obvious form letter. He didn't even try to disguise it, expanding the text of the web-scraped job description.
- He can't honestly suggest that he can "perform the job effectively" without knowing anything about what the job entails.

Now compare that atrocity to this positive example I made up:

```
Dear Mr. Lester,

My colleague Richard Dice referred me to the job recently
posted on jobs.perl.org.  I believe that I can help Elsinore
Brewery with my skills, including:

* Four years of database app development, including...

* Three years Perl experience, including two CPAN modules
    (http://...) that extend the DBI database layer by...

* A BS in computer science from the University of Illinois.

I'm also a bit of an amateur zymurgist and have brewed beer in
my basement for the past five years.

I look forward for a chance to meet with you to discuss
your needs and how I can help you and Elsinore Brewery.

Sincerely,
Bob McKenzie
```

Note how this letter hits all the good points of a cover letter:

- Introduces the writer to the reader and establishes a connection to a mutual friend

- Shows that the writer is familiar with the company and is interested in this specific job

- Summarizes his work experience, perhaps even repeating the summary from the résumé, to explain the key benefits of hiring him

Don't get too tricky in your cover letter. It's good to make a personal connection, but without giving up too much information (refer to Chapter 10, *Too Much Information*, on page 183). Consider that the cover letter is going to color how you're perceived from that point forward. It is your introduction to the company.

Consider how you'll be remembered.

Take a look at this excerpt from a cover letter I received. The candidate didn't have a strong programming background, so he explained other parts of his varied background that might bring value to the position:

> I am much more than a programmer. In my long and varied work history, I have performed such jobs as knife salesman, manager of a hardware store, a neurological lab assistant who was responsible for extracting retinas from bovine eyes, flower delivery driver, and retirement home activities director, all of which make me a well-rounded candidate.

It might be a decent strategy. He's showing he has a wide variety of experiences in his background. But when you read that, what sticks in your mind?

> "I am much more than a programmer. In my long and varied work history, I have performed such jobs as knife salesman, manager of a hardware store, **a neurological lab assistant who was responsible for extracting retinas from bovine eyes**, and...blah blah blah...." Holy cow, this guy was a *cow eye sucker!*.

How do you get past that? From that point on, it's all I could think about. If I actually hired him, he'd forever be known as the cow eye sucker guy.

Your cover letter must keep your benefit to the company at the forefront. It may be appropriate to mention what your goals are, but that must be kept secondary to what the company needs. I've seen too many cover letters like this:

> I saw your ad for a Windows system administrator in the *Herald* this weekend, and I knew I had to respond. I've been looking for a Windows admin position near Poughkeepsie, and this job sounds perfect for me.

There's nothing wrong with discussing what attracted you to the job in the cover letter, so long as it is discussed as of secondary importance to what the company is looking for. In the previous case, the writer is most concerned with how easy his commute would be, with no mention of the benefits to the company. Mentioning the commute is fine, so long as it as at the end of the cover letter, after the company's needs have been discussed.

6.3 Put the Package Together

What you send as you apply for a job will vary, but the overriding rule is "Follow all directions exactly." When the job ad says, "Please send a cover letter and résumé in Word format to...," then by golly you send a cover letter and résumé in Word format. Don't substitute a PDF for Word or put it all in plain text because you think that's what makes more sense. The company specified Word for a reason, and their reason trumps any you might have.

If the ad doesn't specify how you should apply, assume this:

- You'll send a cover letter in a plain-text email, with the name of the position in the Subject field.
- Your résumé attached to the email as a file attachment in either Microsoft Word or PDF format, with your name in the filename, such as bob-smith-resume.pdf.

File naming is important because it helps the résumé weeder keep track of the attachments. It may be meaningful to you on your machine to have a file called resume.pdf, but consider the recipient who has a dozen files all named resume.pdf.

Name file attachments to make life easier for the recipient.

Most important, if you don't do exactly what an ad tells you to do, the employer will know, and what they'll know is "This person is unable to fulfill his first task as assigned." Don't screw it up.

There's one exception to following the ad's instructions, and that's in sending a salary history: don't do it.

6.4 Never Tell Anyone Your Salary History

Somewhere along the line, you may be asked what you were making at your last job. Don't give out that information. When a company is asking for your salary history, they're looking to make an easy decision based on the information, and it is never to your advantage.

Say you're applying for a job where most of the other sysadmins are getting paid $70,000/year. If they company knows you're making $80,000 now, chances are you'll be out of the running immediately. If they know you make $60,000, the hiring manager may think, "This guy will probably take $65,000 and be happy with it, and we can save $5,000." You'll wind up making less than you're worth. Then, when you find out you're underpaid, you leave the company unhappy. Nobody wins.

Don't feel guilty at declining a request for salary history. You are under no obligation to do so. Sometimes an employer will say "We have to have an idea what to pay you," but that's just crap. Here are some reasons why:

- The value to the company of work to be done by you cannot be determined by what someone else paid you.
- Previous salary is a terrible indicator of potential future value.
- Your previous compensation might not have been all salary.
- You could have been underpaid or overpaid at your last job.
- Your reasons for wanting a change in pay are your own business.
- Giving out salary history makes it tempting to lie to make some more money.

Isn't It Rude to Say "That's Confidential?"

Saying "My salary history is confidential" may feel rude, but it's absolutely not. Our society has just trained us to think that everything is everyone else's business.

To many Americans, the idea of keeping things private may seem strange. We live in a society where "reality" TV shows purport to show private details of their subjects' lives. Political discourse can revolve around details of sexual escapades of politicians.

Online, many treat their lives as an open book. Our Twitter updates may announce a trip to the bathroom. A co-worker might discuss his recent surgery over lunch. Single people get asked "So, when are you getting married?" And married people get "When are you having kids?" There seems to be no line of privacy that someone won't cross.

Therefore, it might feel strange, even rude, to turn down a request for information about ourselves. Everything else in the job process is out in the open, so how can you explain that you won't tell someone what you were making at your last three jobs? Don't think of it as "private" but as "confidential."

"Confidential" lends an official air to your refusal. It's almost as if you're saying "Rules outside of my control prevent me from saying." You need not explain that they're rules you've imposed yourself.

There's a simple way to avoid this mess. Tell anyone who asks, "I'm sorry, but that's confidential."

The word *confidential* can be your armor against questions you're not going to answer. If pushed as to why it's confidential, you need only say, "That's not something I discuss with anyone." It's a perfectly polite answer, and you need to be firm about it. Practice it if necessary. Chances are good you'll be asked, and it's best to be prepared. Giving up your salary history never is to your advantage, so be strong and ready when the question comes.

The specifics of declining a request for a salary history, or indeed past pay stubs as proof of your salary history, depend on the request.

Answer a request for salary history with a salary expectation.

If a job ad says, for example, "send résumé and salary history to...," then send your résumé and cover letter as you would any other job. In the cover letter, include a paragraph at the bottom saying "My salary history is confidential. Based on my understanding of the position, the current job market, and experience and talents, I'm expecting that a salary between $X,000 and $Y,000 per year will be appropriate." Note that you're specifically declining the request for salary history, because you don't want the recipient to think that you didn't notice it. You're standing on principle, not being sloppy.

If you have to fill out an employment form and a box asks for your pay rate at each of your last three jobs, write "Confidential." Alternately, you can cross out "Salary Received" and replace with "Salary Expected" and list your salary requirements.

If asked in an interview, do the same as you would in the earlier cover letter. Explain that "I'm sorry, but my salary history is confidential. Based on my understanding of...." Remember to be polite but firm.

You can always discuss your salary requirements when asked. At some point, the topic of salary is going to come up.[1] You can discuss your salary expectations, but not your salary history. The history is nobody's business but yours, while your expectations are the very topic at hand.

But what if they insist? What if the interviewer says "It's our policy that we have to have salary history as part of the process"? What if the ad says "Résumés without salary history will not be considered"?

---

1. See Section 11.5, *Negotiate the Offer*, on page 203 for more about salary negotiations.

Well, what if they do? They're telling you that their hiring procedures revolve around making sure that they have the upper hand in salary negotiations. Is that a company you want to work for? Either you can do what they want and start the hiring process at a disadvantage, instead of as partners working together, or you can find another company. The choice is up to you.

6.5 And Now You Keep Looking

Now you've sent off your email, or faxed a résumé, to the job of your dreams. Now what?

You keep looking. Nothing has changed until you get an interview, get an offer, and accept a new job.

Don't sit by the calendar, counting the days since you sent off your magic email, trying to figure out how long it will take them to get back to you. Keep plugging on looking for a new job.

If you don't get an acknowledgment of receipt of your résumé and cover letter within, say, a week or two, you can go ahead and send a follow-up letter asking for confirmation. However, once you've received confirmation that your résumé has arrived safely, don't follow up again. If they want you, they'll contact you. Not hearing back from an employer may mean they're not interested or that they haven't gotten around to going through résumés yet. In either case, let it lie.

Of course, you hope you'll get contacted for an interview, and preparing for that interview is the subject of our next chapter.

Part II

The Interview and Beyond

Chapter 7

Preparing for the Interview

Since your job interview is your first day at your new job, it only makes sense that you'd want to prepare for it. You wouldn't roll out a new software package without preparation or make server changes without adequately testing, and so too it must be with your job interview.

Your assignment at your job interview is twofold: show the hiring manager that you are the person for the job, and verify to yourself that this is the job you want.

The first thing you must project, however, is that you are prepared for the interview. The interviewer is spending a lot of his time preparing for this interview, and it's critically important that you make clear that you take it as seriously, and it is as of much importance, as he does.

Here's the minimum you need to prepare for the interview:

- Clear your schedule.
- Prepare to sell the interviewer on you.
- Prepare to answer tough questions.
- Prepare your own questions to ask.
- Prepare a relevant portfolio.
- Prepare to get to the interview.
- Prepare the things you're going to take with you.

7.1 Clear Your Schedule

 Here's a scenario for flushing your job prospects away: the interview's going great, the hiring manager seems to enjoy your work, there's real interest on both parties, but then "Gosh I'd love to meet the president of the company, but my baby-sitter is only able to stay until 5 p.m."

Treat your interview like it's the only thing that matters in life, because right then it is. Don't be worrying about time constraints. Just clear your schedule so you can put all your attention on the interview. Not only is watching the clock rude, but it also means you're not going to be 100 percent for the interview. Plus, if the interview runs long, that's usually a *good* thing, because they're interested in you.

7.2 Prepare to Sell the Interviewer on You

You've already thought about being the right person for the job because you submitted a résumé tailor-made for the job in question and a cover letter that's personalized about you and your fit with the company. That's a start, but the amount of information you can convey in a one- or two-page résumé and a cover letter is pretty small. The conversations at your interview will be far larger than that. All the detail you had to leave off your résumé about the death march project you saved from ruin or the network upgrade you pulled off will probably be the meat of the conversation.

Remember always that it *is* a conversation. You aren't just answering questions like a suspect hauled in for police questioning, even if it feels like that. In fact, sitting quietly and only answering what's been asked is an ideal way to lose the interview by showing the interviewer that you have no thoughts of your own or that you're too afraid to speak to her.

7.3 Prepare to Answer Tough Questions

You're going to be answering questions, and they're not all going to be simple "Do you know Unix?" See Chapter 9, *Handling the Tough Interview Questions*, on page 163 for in-depth discussion of these and others, but at the very least be able to answer the following questions *as they relate to the specific job and company*:

- Tell me about yourself.
- What do you know about our company?
- What is your greatest strength?
- What is your greatest weakness?
- Why do you want to work for us?
- Why should we hire you?
- Where do you see yourself in five years?

You're going to get every one of these questions, or a variant of them, in the interview. Know how you're going to answer.

7.4 Prepare a Relevant Portfolio

Imagine a restaurant owner hiring a chef. The owner grills the candidate on his skills, asking "Can you make chicken pot pie?"

"Oh, sure, no problem," he replies.

"How's your lasagna? Enchiladas? Pad thai?"

"Fantastic, without peer!"

"Can you make baklava?"

"Butter soft and flaky!"

"Great! You're hired!"

How can the restaurant owner possibly know the chef can cook what he says he can? More important, why would you hire a chef without tasting his cooking?

Now turn that into a programmer interviewing for a job. The hiring manager asks, "You can do Perl, right? Perl objects? How about SOAP? DNS queries? Third normal form database structures? Recursive descent parsing?"

"Done 'em all."

"Do you write clean code? Good documentation?"

"Oh, of course!"

"Great! You're hired!"

As absurd as it was for the restaurant owner to take the chef's word at face value about his skill, it's absurd for hiring managers to hire without seeing the candidate's skills in action. In the hiring process, however, it can be effectively impossible to demonstrate your skills. While the smart chef might bring an array of dishes to taste, a sysadmin isn't going to be able to create a thousand-node network on demand.

A hiring manager who wants to get a real feel for her candidates' skills will ask for examples of work. When I was hiring programmers, I told every candidate that I called in for a face-to-face interview to bring in code samples, printed on paper, so that we could discuss them during the interview. Unfortunately, I was definitely in the minority. Ilya Talman, one of the top technical recruiters in Chicago, told me that he estimates only 15 percent of hiring managers ask to see samples of work.

This gives you, the pragmatic job hunter, an edge. You're going to bring work samples, even if you're not asked for them.

Use examples of your work to gain an edge over other candidates. Imagine two programmers interviewing for the same position, with the same skills, and equally suited for the work to be done. Now imagine that the second programmer is able to show the hiring manager examples of relevant work that apply to her specific needs. She'll pick the candidate who is able to show what he's done, because she can be more confident in the quality of his work and that he's actually done what he claims to have done.

Bringing sample work gives a strong message that you're serious about this job and that you've committed time and energy to the process. You've created a work product in itself, well prepared for your first day on the job.

Even if the hiring manager doesn't ask for sample work, bring some anyway. You want to stand above all the other candidates, and in an environment where such deliverables aren't expected, a portfolio puts you head and shoulders above the competition. If two project managers are being considered for a position and their skills are roughly the same but one has an attractive, comprehensive portfolio of his work, with actual project schedules, requirements documents, and post-project evaluations, who's going to get the job?

What Goes in My Portfolio?

Unlike your résumé that *tells* how great you are for the job, a portfolio *shows* it. It will be filled with examples of your work, as well as documentation of your working past. The portfolio will help the hiring manager *understand* what you've done in the past and how you'll help her company moving forward.

The work that you bring should relate to the job you're interviewing for, but don't limit yourself. For a Java database programmer job, you'll want to bring code that shows your Java and database chops, but don't stop there. Include some Ruby code, maybe some cool command-line utilities, and some low-level C code for graphics manipulation you did for a game. Bring database schemas you've created and documentation you've written. Show *depth* of experience in Java database programming but *breadth* of experience elsewhere.

Your portfolio must showcase your best work. Don't bring in something that can't stand on its own. Too often I've looked through a candidate's sample code only to have it disclaimed: "Oh, that's just a little shell script I had to write once for doing some backups." If you're not proud of it, don't bring it.

Here are examples of work products to bring:

- Source code listings (syntax highlighting can make things easier to read):
- Screenshots
- Network diagrams
- Disaster recovery plans, backup plans, and so on
- Database schemas
- Documentation
- Project schedules
- Websites, both screens and HTML code

If you have work products that cross functional boundaries, include them! Sysadmins who have written impressive shell scripts should definitely include them. Programmers who can draft project schedules should include those, and so on.

These work products should be created solely by you or else prominently disclaimed in writing. Something as simple as "Written with another sysadmin" at the top of the first page of the document should be fine. The key is that you don't want it to come back that you misrepresented the work as being only yours if it's not.

Of course, never bring anything proprietary or confidential. For some things like source code, this can be a sticking point, whereas for a project schedule it might be less so. You want to highlight your abilities, not get yourself a lawsuit.

Open source work is ideal for your portfolio. One way to make sure you don't run afoul of confidentiality issues is to stock your portfolio with contributions you've made to open source projects. If you've contributed only parts of code to an open source project, print out the parts you've done, and denote them as such. Remember that your contributions might not just be code but could include documentation, design plans, schedules...whatever.

Portfolios can also include nontechnical documents, such as:

- Performance reviews, with any mentions of salary redacted
- Letters of recommendation
- Any assessment of your work, such as blog postings about an open source project you worked on

As with the technical documentation, make sure nothing is proprietary.

Construct Your Portfolio

The ideal portfolio will be a three-ring binder with your name and contact information on the front. The pages will be divided into sections with labeled tab dividers to make it easy to find content later. You want to leave it behind with the hiring manager so she can refer to it later while pondering your awesomeness and so she can show others.

Knowing that you may have to create multiple portfolios for future interviews, I suggest you create one master portfolio with all your possible content and then make copies from those when you have a portfolio to create. You can easily pick and choose from what in your background is relevant to the job you're applying for.

The portfolio, even a humble three-ring binder, should still be a quality job. You don't need to have any fancy square-binding, but it should still look neat. The info page you put on the front should look neat and professional, just like your résumé.

As you put together the pages that go into the binder, it's better to err on the side of too many examples than too few. The tabbed dividers will make it easy for the reader to find what's interesting. On the other hand, don't overwhelm the reader with paper. You don't want to include 100 pages of some database abstraction library you wrote, just for the sake of completeness. The first ten to fifteen pages will probably be enough to show the reader what you're capable of.

When you're done putting it all together, stick in one final page as the first page: a copy of your résumé.

Create New Work for the Portfolio

Sometimes the best item in a portfolio isn't existing work at all. You may want to look at creating something specific for a given interview. Consider my friend Kate's story:

Kate's Quick Reference Card
by Kate Thieda, independent business owner, Durham, North Carolina

I applied to a tech company as a production manager for their main product, quick reference cards for programmers, but I was discouraged. After over a year of frustrating job searching, I had almost given up. I knew that with the fierce competitiveness for jobs, I had to do something to stand out from all the other candidates.

I decided to make my own cheat sheet, using the look and feel of the company's product. I followed their formatting as closely as possible and filled it with information about myself, a sort of a "cheat sheet" for them to remember me and my qualifications after the interview. I listed all my skills relevant to the position, quotes from my supervisors from performance reviews, and other tidbits that mirrored what they had on each of their cards. As

> with all interviews, one of the first questions was, "Tell us why
> you think you'd be good for this job." I pulled out the card, and
> they had the answer in their hands. Two days later, I got the job.

Consider the impression that must have made with that version
of the company's product that related exactly to her. In a few
hours of work, Kate created something that said she was familiar with the company and what it did, she had an eye for detail,
she wanted *that job*, and she was willing to go above and beyond
the normal expectations of a candidate to get it. It's no wonder
they hired her.

Do I Really Have to Do All This?

It depends on you. Do you really want this job? Do you want
to separate yourself from the guy after you who doesn't have a
portfolio?

Beyond showing quality work, a portfolio says, "I want *this* job."
The message is inescapable. The cost of a portfolio might be a
few hours of time and maybe $10 of photocopying and supplies
at an office-supply store. You'd be hard-pressed to find a better
return on your investment.

7.5 Prepare Your Questions to Ask

Since the job interview is a two-way process, you should have
questions for the interviewer and potentially for other people
there who aren't your manager-to-be. In fact, a candidate who
doesn't have questions during the interview raises a number of
questions with his silence: "Does he not care about what the
job will be like?" "Is she not interested in this job?" "Maybe he
thinks this job is just another stepping stone to something else."
"Seems like she can't be bothered to think ahead about how this
job might work out."

Asking questions shows that you're interested in the position
and that you're not cruising through life. The interviewer has
invested time and energy in getting you into the interview room,
and it's a nail in your coffin to give the impression that you're
not being interested in determining whether the position you're
applying for is appropriate.

Always take a list of questions with you to each interview. Most interviewers will be happy to answer questions throughout the interview, provided that they are relevant to the current discussion.

Hiring manager: *...and so our work day is typically 8 a.m. to 5 p.m., although of course there are times we need to work longer.*

You: *Absolutely, these things can come up. How often is that, typically?*

Some interviewers may not like to have their flow interrupted. If you ask a question and it seems unwelcome, thank the interviewer for the answer after he's finished, check it off your list, and save the rest for the end.

You need to be careful when asking some of the questions that relate to you and what you can expect out of the job. You want to keep emphasis in the interview about the company and how you'll help it, but it's OK to ask about the day-to-day technical aspects of the job. Absolutely do not ask about salary or benefits. That is for a job offer.

If in your interview a question on your list is answered, then make a check mark on the list. When the interviewer asks at the end if you have any questions, you can refer to your list and ask. If at the end of it all, all your questions have been answered, you can still recap the questions you had and what the answers were.

Hiring manager: *Do you have any questions for me?*

You: *Let's see, you talked about the workday being 8 a.m. to 5 p.m. and talked about the benefits program. Does the company contribute to any open source projects?*

Even if all your questions were answered in the course of the interview, show that you came prepared by recapping your answered questions.

Don't have a stock set of questions you ask at every interview. The questions you ask should reflect your interest in the company and make it clear that you have researched the company and have really thought about the interview process. For example, you might ask, "What kinds of challenges have you had selling a product that's available as open source?" or "How do you sell books to the school market when everyone already knows about Amazon.com?"

It's OK to ask questions about things that relate to you, but also ask some that make it clear that you're thinking about the benefits you can bring to the company. If everything you ask is about vacation and working hours and whether you're going to have to wear a tie, it's going to be off-putting to the interviewer. Find a balance between your personal concerns and questions about the company.

Finally, make sure that your list is written down, even printed. No matter how good your memory is, when you're on the hot seat, you're likely to forget. Don't be embarrassed to bring in a sheet of paper with questions. Indeed, it shows your preparedness.

What Will a Day Be Like?

You want to know what's going to be expected of you day to day. Many other questions may build off of this. Two very different answers from two different programming managers may be as follows:

Hiring manager: *Every Monday we have our 9-to-11 staff meeting that all eighteen of us attend. Sometimes it runs into lunch. It's where I explain what we'll be doing the coming week and lay out performance goals for everyone. Other days, I expect that everyone is at work at 9 a.m. sharp. Lunch is from 12:30 to 1. End of the day is at 5, and I expect a recap of the day's events before everyone leaves.*

Or you might get this:

Hiring manager: *Around 9 a.m. most days the project teams have a five-minute stand-up meeting to start the day. We've found that this helps everyone get in sync with the people who matter most, and it helps clear out the morning cobwebs. Different teams have different styles. Some do pair programming, and some work solo. It really depends on who's on the individual team.*

The first manager is clearly interested in making sure things run according to a specific set of rules. He's very much into command and control. The second is more likely to let things happen however they happen. Neither answer is better or worse other than for what's important to you.

What Are the Hours Like? How Often Are You Working Overtime? Weekends?

This can be touchy, because you don't want to come across like a lazy, self-serving jerk. However, there's nothing wrong with wanting to know what will be expected. It's best to simply ask and note the answer, without comment. The time to negotiate the parts of the job that you don't like are after you have a job offer, not before.

Remember that you're not there to give the interviewer your problems, so avoid this:

You: *How much overtime is there? I've got a bowling league on Wednesdays, and sometimes I have to pick up my grandma to take her to get hair done at Field's on Saturday mornings; she's been going there for more than thirty years, you know....*

However, there are cases where there may be a definite need that must be addressed and should be discussed forthrightly. I once interviewed a programmer who was an Orthodox Jew and had to be home on Fridays before sundown (see Section 10.1, *Religious Affiliations*, on page 185 for details). If he'd turned out to have been qualified for the position, I'd have found a way to work around this scheduling limitation. Different situations may not have that flexibility.

This is also a great example of being a right fit for the company. This man's faith was paramount to him, and a company that required him to work outside the restrictions of his faith would not have been right for him.

This is also an example of a rare case where it's appropriate to discuss religion in the workplace.

What Sorts of Projects Will I Be Working On? What Do You See Me Working on My First Week? Month? Year?

You need to know what sorts of things will be expected of you, to know how it fits your style.

A big red flag is if the manager doesn't have an answer, like this manager interviewing a sysadmin:

Hiring manager: *I'm not really sure right now. I know that Dave needs some help with day-to-day operations over on the database side, but I haven't worked that out just yet. He's doing Oracle, or maybe it's DB2 now.*

It's far better to get an answer like this:

Hiring manager: *Right now, I've got to get our backups under control. They're taking six hours overnight, and when they run past 8 a.m., it really affects system throughput for all the Oracle users. So, the first thing I need is to have you implement an automated backup server, probably a jukebox. After that, we need to upgrade to Oracle 10 for our main development server. I can't let you keep this, but here's a look at our plan for the rest of the fiscal year....*

The second manager has told you a lot. She's on top of the company's IT needs, and she has plans for the future. Most important, you're probably not going to be sitting around twiddling your thumbs on your first day. She's probably a good person to work for.

Is This a New Position, or Is It Replacing Someone?

If the position is a new one, then there's growth in the department. Follow up by asking how much growth is planned.

If you'd be replacing someone, ask to hear about that person, such as "Tell me about Dave. What did he bring to the company?" It should give you some idea of the shoes you'd be likely to fill if the previous employee was highly regarded or what to avoid if not. Note that you're not asking for dirty details of Dave's departure but giving the interviewer room to tell if he chooses.

Tell Me About the Team I'd Be Joining

This shows that you're serious about getting along with others, as well as giving you background to decide whether it's a team you'd want to join. If the hiring manager doesn't give much of an idea of how the team interacts, dig further with "Does everyone eat lunch together" or "Do people on the team hang out after work?" As always, there's no right or wrong answer that you want to hear back from the interviewer, but those two questions will likely get at the core of what you want to know.

Other Questions You May Want to Ask

The previous questions are just a start to give you an idea of questions that may aid with your assessment of the company and that help show that you're engaged in the interview and think like a businessperson. Here are some others:

- How much interaction with the rest of the company is there?
- What has turnover been like in the department? The company?
- What are the future plans for the department? The company?
- How many positions are you hiring for?
- How do I deal with outside projects?
- Are there prohibitions on outside projects? Is there some sort of intellectual property agreement?
- Do you use open source software? Do you contribute to open source? How? Are there restrictions?
- How long have you been here? Tell me about your time at the company.
- How do you like it here?
- What would you do differently if you could?
- What challenges is the company facing? The department?
- How do you do performance reviews?
- Who do I report to? Who does she report to? What's the org chart look like?

7.6 Prepare to Get to the Interview

All your preparation goes down the toilet if you're late for the interview. Being late is, for most interviewers, a black mark from which you are unlikely to recover in the job race. Make sure you can get to the interview in plenty of time.

First, find where you're going, *before* the day of the interview, so you have plenty of time to plan. Take into account all of these factors when planning your trip.

- Is it in an unfamiliar city? Or a part of the city you don't know?

- What's traffic like at that time of day?

- Is there construction?

- Will you have to find parking?

- Is it in a big building? You may wind up taking ten minutes between the ground floor and the company's offices from elevator congestion.

Coming into the interview saying "Aw, man, sorry I'm late; traffic was *so* bad" won't let you off the hook. The hiring manager can get to work on time, so you can, too.

The best way to plan is to make a practice trip. If you're driving, drive to the interview the day before, at the same time that the interview will be, so you can see for yourself what traffic and parking are like.

Leave yourself an extra 25 to 50 percent of your estimated time to get there as buffer time. Bring a book to read in the parking lot or a nearby coffee shop in case everything goes right and you have time to kill. Better still, go over your questions, portfolio, and notes about the company, so you're as prepared as can be.

7.7 Prepare What You're Going to Bring with You

Get ready early for the interview. Don't sink the interview by bringing the wrong things and showing up late. Here's the start of a checklist:

- At least five extra copies of your résumé: Make sure it's the one that's tailored to the company. You'll refer to it during the interview, and the interviewer may not have his copy handy. And you'll want to give one to various people you meet.

- Pen and paper: You're going to have to fill out forms, and you're going to be taking notes.

- Directions and a map: Even if you drove it already or you're sure you know where the place is, bring printed directions in case you get lost or confused.

- A full tank of gas: You'll have enough to worry about on the way to the interview without being concerned about running on empty.

- Comb, makeup, and so on: For last-minute touch-ups in the parking lot or the lobby restroom.

- A bottle of water: You may want to bring a small bottle of water, if you're discreet about it. Talking for hours tends to make one thirsty.

This list is not all-inclusive but is meant to give you ideas. It's all about being prepared and how you do that best is up to you.

What Not to Bring

Then there are things you're just not going to have with you, lest they distract from your all-important business meeting.

- Any other person: This includes parents, spouses, children, whatever. The interview is your show, and anyone else is a distraction, even if you think they're going to wait in the lobby. See Section 7.1, *Clear Your Schedule*, on page 124 for more.

- Gum or cigarettes: You're not going to chew gum or smoke. Even if you think you can get away with a cig outside before the interview, you're going to smell like smoke. Don't do it.

- Food or drink: The last thing you need is coffee spilled down your shirt or crumbs on your skirt.

- An unsilenced cell phone: Few things are ruder than a phone call in the middle of the interview. Make sure it's silenced, or leave it in the car. What phone call could you be expecting that's more important than the job interview?

In all these examples, note that the two goals are to present yourself the best way possible and shut out all noninterview distractions.

7.8 Preparation Is Half the Battle

Preparing for the interview is the best way to improve your chances of landing the job. When you're well-prepared, you'll be calmer, and you'll enjoy the process more. When you're calmer, you'll do better.

Preparing for the interview also means that you will *look like* you prepared for the interview. When you're fumbling for answers or paperwork in the interview seat, it leaves a bad impression with the interviewer.

Finally, after you've read the next chapter, Chapter 8, *The Interview*, on the next page, come back and revisit this chapter in light of any new ideas you pick up from there. That chapter and this go hand in hand.

The Interview

Many people hate job interviews, and you may be one of them. You feel like you're on trial, or you're being interrogated. You're afraid of making a mistake. You're afraid of not knowing the answer to a question or of giving the wrong answer to a question and losing the job.

Others feel more nonchalant, where they sit and politely answer the questions and have a sort of *que sera sera* attitude. Whatever happens happens, so there's really not much to worry about, right?

Neither approach is a good one.

The hiring manager *wants to hire you.* She wants you to be the one candidate to solve her problems, to end her quest for the perfect candidate. She wouldn't

> The hiring manager wants to hire you.

have brought you in if she didn't think that you could be that candidate. She would rather being working on projects, helping the company make money, than interviewing yet another candidate.

An interview can be as draining on her as it is for you. Each interview eats up hours of her day, and the hiring process is expensive. Nobody does it just for fun.

For the nonchalant, leaving your fate in the hands of others is counterproductive. Not only is it a sad way to go through life, but it will come through in your interview. No one wants a programmer, a system administrator, or a tester who is unable to take charge of the problems facing him. You have to show the hiring manager that you are the best person for this job. You must be an active participant in the interview if you're to have a real chance of getting hired.

> **The interview is your first day of your new job.**

No matter your outlook, always remember that a job interview is a business meeting with the potential employer. Just as your résumé is your first work product for your new employer, your interviews are your first business meetings. They're also about you, as the candidate, interviewing your prospective new employer about things that are important to you. Both parties come to the table as equals.

When you come to the interview prepared, as discussed in the previous chapter and ready to answer the tough questions, which I'll discuss in the next, you won't feel so much like you're on trial, and you'll be ready to take control and present the best face possible.

8.1 Work Toward Your Goal of Getting an Offer

Your primary goal at a job interview is simple: get a job offer, or move to the next step in the process to getting a job offer. Chances are you won't get offered a job on the spot, but you're there to convince those you meet that you're the best fit for the job. You want to impress them enough that when the decisions are made in the hours or days after your interview, the decision is obvious: offer you a job.

Too often, I've had candidates sit across my desk as if their assignment at a job interview is to show up and answer questions. Certainly, you must show up, and you must answer questions, but that's not sufficient. Compare these two goals: "get a job offer" and "answer questions." Answering questions is passive, leaving you in a subservient position. It's a terrible way to approach the interview. On the other hand, "get a job offer" is active and helps you think of yourself on equal footing with your interviewer. Take charge of what happens, rather than hoping that Fate smiles on you, allowing you to have gainful employment.

Note that "get a job offer" is not "find out details about the offer." You're not there to figure out what you could make, how good the benefits are, or where you're going to sit. Those are for consideration after you have the offer. You can still find things out along those lines, but they are secondary to getting the offer. Without a job offer, the questions of pay and benefits are irrelevant.

8.2 Listen to Everything

There's an old saying: "Listening is twice as important as speaking, so God gave us two ears and one mouth." Even if you wind up doing most of the talking at an interview, the importance of listening can't be overstated.

Interviewers ask questions for a reason. What you're being asked can tell you more about an organization than hours of research. At the very least, you have topics to follow up on later in the interview.

If the hiring manager asks about your skills with the Apache Tomcat application server, it's not because she's pulled buzzwords out of a book called *101 Hot Buzzwords to Ask Job Candidates*. She has tasks and problems, and she wants you to solve them, so you're going to explain how you can help her using your knowledge of Tomcat, if you can. Then, you're going to synthesize that knowledge with what you already know about the organization and can follow up. If it's a Java shop and they're not using Tomcat already, you might ask, "Are you considering a move to Tomcat?" If it's not a Java shop, there's an even wider range of possible reasons. The key is to engage in discussion about your skills and the problems you can solve with them.

> Try to understand the reason for each question asked.

When future peers ask questions, it's an opportunity to learn about the organization in a way that you might not get without working there. Those peers are wanting to make sure that you're not going to cause any problems for them, and their questions will likely reflect that concern. Further, these interviewers are less likely to be...tactful about their queries, and that openness can work to your advantage.

A panel of peers might probe at your coding style, for example. It might be vague, like "Tell us about your coding style," or pointed as in "You're not married to any dogmatic programming style guides, are you?" Clearly, there's something behind the question, so answer their question, and ask your own.

Future peer: *What books have been especially helpful to your programming career?*

You: *I've learned from and been influenced by a number of books, such as Code Complete[1] and Perl Best Practices[2]. I'm especially a fan of Code Complete's take on variable naming. I think every programmer should memorize them. But I've also been around enough to know that once you know the rules, you learn to know when to break them, because life is never as clean as we'd like. Have you guys had problems in the past with stylistic clashes on the team?*

Future peer: *Yeah, well, let's just say that there are those on the team who take a certain book as gospel, no matter what anyone else says or what the project is.*

Others: *<snickers and chuckles>*

One little question turns over a rock of dissension and unhappiness in the team. Note also that it's important to turn over the rock and ask your follow-up question, rather than assuming "Kathy asked about coding style, and the others laughed, so I bet there's a problem there." Don't assume.

You: *Sounds like that has been a problem. How have you handled it?*

Finally, your listening should probably extend to paper, where you write down notes about what's been said. You don't want to derail a conversation in order to write down complete thoughts. A simple "MS Office remote problems" jotted on your notepad may remind you later in the day to bring up your expertise in supporting Microsoft Office with a large distributed sales force.

---

1. *Code Complete [McC04]*
2. *Perl Best Practices [Con05]*

8.3   Treat Each Person Like the CEO

An interview is all about the people. If everything about you could be expressed on a piece of paper and there was no need to interact directly with other humans, there would be no need for this chapter at all.

Pay attention to how you meet people. The old saying of "You never get a second chance to make a first impression" is repeated for a reason. When you meet someone, remind yourself "I need to make a good impression." Shake hands with the person you're meeting, unless physical positioning prevents it, such as with a receptionist sitting behind a desk. Introduce yourself by both first and last name, and explain why you're there.

Someone in the lobby: *May I help you? You look like you're waiting for someone.*

You: *Yes, I'm Susan Candidate. I'm here to meet with Mike Manager.*

This goes for anyone you're introduced to. If it's obvious what's going on, like you're clearly there for an interview, say something about what you've seen so far.

Peter Programmer: *[Sticking his head in manager's office] Mike, just wanted to say that we've started the test load on Muskrat.*

Mike Manager: *Hey, Peter, glad you're here. Susan is interested in the database administrator position, and we were just talking about your project.*

You: *[standing] Hi, Peter, I'm Susan Candidate. [shaking Peter's hand] Mike was saying that Muskrat has some messy legacy data.*

These ad hoc introductions are common. Even if you're only talking to a single manager, you'll run into many other people along the way. You might talk to the receptionist, fill out forms for someone in human resources, and get seen by a half dozen people as you walk to the manager's office. At some point, someone might interrupt the interview to ask a time-critical question.

How to Shake Hands

Shake hands with someone by grasping their hand in yours, your thumb webbing against his or her thumb webbing. Squeeze firmly while you raise and lower your hand once or twice. Then let go. All the while, you should be looking your shaking partner in the eye.

Note that "firm" does not mean "crushing grip," nor does it mean "dainty," "limp," or, worst of all, "dead fish." Women, especially, don't offer the ends of your fingers to be squeezed passively. Be a partner in the handshake.

If you're seated, stand up to shake someone's hand. Traditionally, women have stayed seated to shake hands, but there's no reason not to stand. Stay standing until the other person has taken a seat or left.

Later, the manager might call someone else in to discuss a facet of the job.

> Every person you meet could make or break your chance of getting the job.

Every one of those people is effectively an interviewer. Each person will form an opinion about you and about how you act or speak, and it may reflect on you later in the process, either positively or negatively. You may not have any way of knowing who these people you meet are. That guy in sweats stopping your interviewer for a quick question in the hall just might be the company president. You have to treat everyone as if they could help or hinder your job search.

One other note on getting along with others: don't swear. As you get into the interview, building rapport with your interviewer or others in the company, conversation will become more relaxed. Maybe you'll be exchanging horror stories with the manager, and he'll drop a few four-letter words in his conversation.[3] Don't think "This guy's cool; I don't have to watch myself" and that it's

---

3. There's an old maxim that says "Profanity is the one language all programmers know."

OK to start using profanity. Not everyone you meet with may feel the same way. Stay professional.

8.4 A Walk Through the Interview

There are as many different interviews as there are companies that hire people. Your interview might be one-on-one, as part of a panel, over the phone, or at a coffee shop. Certain principles apply no matter what. Let's walk through the interview with these universal principles in mind.

Arriving at the Interview

Arrive at the interview at least ten minutes early, pen in hand. Chances are good that you'll fill out an application or other paperwork before you meet the hiring manager. Allow time for this paperwork before the scheduled start time.

More important, being late for an interview is just about an unforgivable sin. The interviewer's time is valuable, and arriving late is an insult to the person who's there on time. You're saying "My time is more valuable than yours." Arrive early to make sure this doesn't happen.

Of course, "showing up" means "showing up prepared, both mentally and in what you bring with you," as discussed in Section 7.7, *Prepare What You're Going to Bring with You*, on page 136.

The Receptionist

As you walk in, get a feel for your surroundings. Is there expensive art on the walls in a well-appointed lobby? Is it a startup in a cheap office storefront with beanbag chairs on the floor?

Find the receptionist. If there's not a dedicated person performing the role of a receptionist, the first person you see will effectively be your receptionist. Note that I said the first *person*, not the first *woman*. If you bypass a group of men to speak to a woman, you'll be remembered but not positively.

You must be unfailingly pleasant and polite to this person, because there are no second chances at a first impression.

Chances are the receptionist will have feedback about you to pass on to whomever is involved with hiring you.

After every interview, after the candidate has left the building, I immediately ask the company receptionist for her thoughts, as well as opinions from anyone else he may have met.

Initial Introductions

After a while in the lobby waiting patiently, it's time to meet the interviewer. This is where the real work begins.

When you first meet the interviewer, introduce yourself and shake hands if offered. There may be a bit of small talk, and you should find out what you're going to be doing at the interview and who you'll be meeting with.

Interviewer: *Hi, Steve? I'm Todd Trainer, and I'm one of the recruiting specialists in HR. I trust you found us OK?*

You: *Hi, Todd, I'm glad to meet you. Thanks for taking the time to meet with me today. The directions on the website were great, and I checked Google Maps as backup. I take it I'll be meeting with Mr. Weston a little later?*

Interviewer: *Yes, the way we like to do things is that you and I will be getting some paperwork done, and I'll explain a little about Conglomco. Then I'll take you to meet with some of Bob's staff, and at 11 you'll be meeting with Bob in his office.*

Note that everything is fine, no matter what. Do not give into the temptation to gripe to say, "Yeah, the directions were fine; I'm just glad I got here through all the traffic!" Nobody wants a griper, even in tiny doses.

As you're being told about the plans for the interview, don't be afraid to write them down. You're likely to forget something, and it's better to be able to refer to "Mr. Trainer"[4] instead of "the man who met me out in the lobby, from HR I think?" Keeping notes is a good sign, because it says you're actually interested in what's happening and doing a good job at it.

---

4. Always refer to each person as Mr. or Ms. Lastname unless the person specifically says to call him or her by another name.

On the other hand, writing everything down can come across as antisocial or more concerned with the notes than with the conversation. You want to take notes, not court testimony. Also, it's polite to ask whether anyone objects to your taking notes.

Opening the Interview

The interviewer will probably open with a little background about the company, explain what they do, and maybe discuss the industry if it's new to you. He'll talk about the department's role and responsibilities in the company. Listen. Listen very carefully, because this is what you must address. Make regular notes so that you don't forget what it is you wanted to discuss or ask about and so that you don't spend all your brain cells remembering what you wanted to say, instead of using them to listen to what is being said.

The interviewer will probably give you a chance to discuss your-self, your history, and your skills in an introductory way. He may say "How's the job search going?" or "You've got a lot of different experience here," or even leave it wide open with "So, tell me about yourself." This is where you lay out a brief history of yourself, highlighting the most important skills you offer, *as they relate to the company.*

Interviewer: *...so with the offshore competition, management is watching costs like crazy, but the merger still leaves us almost doubling the number of users we have to support. But enough about us, tell me about you.*

You: *Well, after I graduated from Northwestern with a degree in computer science and a minor in business, I spent a few years working various system administration jobs, getting my feet wet, and getting exposed to as many different operating environments as I could. Those are the bottom three jobs on my résumé. The last four years I've been working for Parsleytronic, working on integrating Windows and Solaris environments. Integrating the sales and engineering sides of Parsleytronic, with only a minor increase in the IT budget, sounds a lot like what you're going through with your merger. How has the merging of the companies' IT departments been going?*

Note how you're answering the question and showing your past experience with something similar to the job you're applying for, if not exactly the same. You've recapped the high points of your résumé, even though they're on the résumé already. Maybe he never noticed that minor in business before. Maybe your résumé wasn't clear enough that you were integrating Windows and Solaris. The recap helps make sure your points are made.

Somehow you want to tie yourself to the needs of the company and the hiring manager, even if only to just show interest in what's going on. Maybe your background isn't as good a fit as in the previous example, but you're not out of luck.

You: *...and then I've been at ShmooCo since 2004 working on engineering applications for brake subsystems. I've certainly had my share of challenges in my past, but your merging of the departments sounds like a big one. I'd like to hear more about how that's going.*

I'm sure there's a skeptic reading this saying "Boy, that would make you sound like a total suck-up." It would if it were insincere, but it won't be. You're going to be very interested on your first day of paid employment, right? So, be interested right now at your first meeting with your potential new boss. If you're *not* interested in the hiring manager's company, his problems, or his concerns, then you're in the wrong interview.

We'll delve further into how to open the interview in Section 9.4, *Tell Me About Yourself*, on page 166.

8.5 Sell Yourself by Telling Stories

Getting the job offer requires selling yourself. It's the active part of "get a job offer," and it's what can make the difference between getting the job you want and losing out to someone who took the time to do the right kind of selling.

Selling yourself isn't evil, it isn't creepy, and you don't have to feel like a used-car salesman. It's just putting forth the information about yourself that the interviewer may not know. If the interviewer never asks about your hot skills in automated testing, project estimation, or administering web server clusters, it's your responsibility to bring them up.

Don't assume that because a given skill is listed on your résumé that the interviewer will delve into it in the interview. The interviewer has probably not memorized the entire thing, no matter how interested she is in you. In fact, the things that stick out in her mind are the items that she sees as important, and you may be able to raise awareness of the other good aspects of your background.

Bring up skills that show you in your best light.

The core of selling yourself is telling stories, preferably specific, quantifiable stories that don't fit on your résumé. Instead of answering questions as simple, matter-of-fact yes-no exchanges, like so:

Interviewer: *Do you know Perl's testing framework?*

Weak answer: *Sure, we use it all the time.*

turn the question into a jumping point for you to tell a story about the topic:

Strong answer: *Yes, very well. I started out using Test::More when I was writing my own CPAN modules, just testing the module I'd written. From there I wrote my own testing add-on, Test::Wango. Now, we use the Test::More framework and the TAP protocol for testing about one third of our internal applications, and the plan is to be at 100 percent by the end of the year.*

The latter answer shows the depth of your knowledge and opens up a world of discussion. If nothing else, it gives you the opportunity to teach the interviewer something he didn't know himself. Maybe he'd never heard of TAP or never realized that you could test more than modules with Test::More.

He wouldn't have asked, "Do you know the TAP protocol?" because he didn't even know it existed. You may have just shown the interviewer that you are even better at a given area than he or his current staff are, and that's a great position to be in.

The latter answer also gives you a chance to show your enthusiasm for the topic at hand. A good manager loves to see passion and excitement for a topic, and that first bland answer just doesn't expose any. Selling yourself is about answering more

> ### Don't Play the RTFM Game with Your Résumé
>
> RTFM means "Read the Freaking Manual," often said to someone online who has asked a question where an answer to that question happens to exist elsewhere. It's an attitude that will crush your chances at getting a good job, as well as getting along with others.
>
> Tech people often think "If someone asks me about what has already been written, it's an imposition or even an insult," They're not afraid to let that attitude show. The thing is, people will see you as a jerk, which is the last thing you want.
>
> Maybe an interviewer will ask "You know Oracle, right?" If your response is "Yeah, it's right there on my résumé," you're saying "RTFM." RTFM assumes that the person is stupid or lazy. Your interviewer is neither.
>
> Maybe he just missed the Oracle part. Maybe he barely skimmed your résumé. Maybe you forgot to put it in there yourself. Putting him on the defensive by pointing out that he missed it serves no one.
>
> You were probably asked "You know Oracle, right?" as an open-ended entry into a conversation about your Oracle skills. Assume this is the case. Come back with "Yes, I've worked with Oracle back at Yoyodyne. We had quite a data warehouse going, although we had some startup problems. Boy, I could tell some horror stories, but I learned a lot. Are you looking to start working with Oracle?"
>
> It's not an annoyance; it's an opportunity to sell yourself.

than the simple question with the information that your interviewer really wants to know, even if he doesn't know it at the time he asks.

Ask Questions

Not only does your boss-to-be need to know whether you're a fit for the company, but it's just as important that you get to know the company and your boss-to-be so that you can decide whether the job is a fit for you. You should ask questions of your interviewer throughout the interview process, when it feels natural in the course of conversation. The questions you ask should also help show your interest in the job.

- "You've said you're moving to all Perl from PHP for your web applications. Why is that, and how is that conversion going?"

- "It seemed pretty crazy out in the programmer office when you showed me around. Is this common? Is there a big project wrapping up?"

- "I notice some books on Oracle on your shelves, but you're a PostgreSQL shop. Are you looking to convert?"

Of course, you'll have a list of questions that you wrote before the interview, as discussed in Section 7.5, *Prepare Your Questions to Ask*, on page 130. If you can work them in conversationally, then mark them off your list as you go. Don't be embarrassed about having a list.

Do not bring up salary or benefits in an interview. That is for the job offer stage and will be discussed at that point. If the interviewer brings up salary or benefits, then follow his lead, but don't probe yourself. Leave discussion of these crucial matters for the offer stage. Your job is to get the offer, not discuss what an offer might contain.

I can't emphasize enough how important it is to leave money out of your interview process. I know it can be aggravating and your patience may be thin and you really want to know how much you're going to make, but don't give in. Don't try to say, "I don't want to waste anyone's time here, so how much is this job paying?" It won't work. At the very least, you'll sound like the money is more important than the work.

Handle Technical Questions

The technical questions will probably be the easiest part of the interview, because they're the most easily answered. Either you know the answer or you don't. When asked about a technical issue, you usually don't want to answer with a simple "yes" or "no," because that's probably not what the interviewer is looking for. You also want to take the time to try to sell yourself a bit.

Interviewer: *Do you know any Ruby?*

Weak answer: *Yeah, some.*

Strong answer: *Some. Back at Peekax Research, we had a little project to decide on a new web framework. I was on the team looking into Rails and got pretty well immersed into some of the dark corners of Ruby. We went with J2EE, but I'd do more Ruby work in a heartbeat.*

You can also see how more detailed answers help eliminate any confusion. The simple answer without evidence is open to misinterpretation. Chances are that what you consider knowing Ruby "some" will not be what the interviewer thinks. Even if the question is about a skill that isn't core to your job, which is likely the case for such a simple question, you don't want to have the problem in the future of misconceptions about your knowledge: "What do you mean you don't know how yield works? You said you knew Ruby!"

As you tell the story about the work, take responsibility for what you did. Don't be vague and mushy about the work that you did and the roles you played. You are selling yourself specifically, not the place that you worked for.

Interviewer: *What work have you done in Ruby?*

Weak answer: *At my current job, we've developed four basic internal CRUD applications in Ruby on Rails, and we even published a package of math functions to RubyForge.*

Strong answer: *I was on a team of three developers who created four CRUD applications in Rails. We'd been using .NET, but I convinced my boss to let us give Ruby a try. I also went through some hoops to get management to let us release one of our math libraries as a gem on RubyForge. It's called Arithmegoo, and it's had a few hundred downloads so far.*

Note the strength of taking responsibility, of saying "I did this." Even as part of a team, you are not an amorphous blob of workers. There are actions that you have taken.

Note also the difference between giving a vague overview and telling a story with details. Details make the story come alive. Details give authority to your words. Details engage the listener.

Be sure to listen to and pay attention to the interviewer. She may not be looking for a long answer. If your tales of how many gems you've published on RubyForge are making the interviewer get that faraway look as she loses interest, cut them short. Of course, this is also true of the entire interview process.

Sometimes the answer to the question is a "no," and you need to basically say that. You never want to pretend you know things that you don't, but you don't have to just say, "No, I don't know about that." Here are three responses that are better than "no," in order of preference.

1. Discuss something you've done similar. "I haven't used LDAP, but back in 2006 at Yoyodyne, I set up and administered Active Directory for a 2,500-person company." Make sure you don't tack on something like "... and LDAP's pretty much the same as Active Directory," with the implication "If you can do LDAP, you can do Active Directory." Maybe the interviewer sees LDAP as vastly inferior to Active Directory. Just provide the facts, not the value judgments.

2. Show that you're at least familiar with the name. "No, I haven't. Are you doing some sort of enterprise-wide directory integration?" You're showing that you have some understanding of how it's used, and you're getting more information. It may turn out that you have a different, similar experience and can turn this into answer 1.

3. Ask what it is and how it's used. "I'm sorry, no, I haven't even heard the term. What is LDAP, and how are you using it?" You'll show interest in learning more, and may find out that it's similar to something you've done before and can upgrade your answer to answer 2.

Please don't use the cliché "No, I don't, but I'm a quick learner!" It's good to try to turn a negative into a positive, but "I'm a quick learner" says nothing.[5] Use one of these three answers.

How to Use Your Portfolio

If you've created a portfolio of work, as discussed in Section 7.4, *Prepare a Relevant Portfolio*, on page 125, use it throughout the

---

5. See Appendix A, on page 235, for more of these clunkers.

Don't Panic!
_____

Don't think of each question as a question that you're doomed for not knowing, to be flung from the bridge for not knowing the airspeed velocity of an unladen swallow. I once asked a candidate, out of the blue, if he knew anything about LDAP. I thought he was going to have a heart attack as he stammered out his "Uh, uh, no, but, uh, I can learn pretty quick!"

Chances are if you've been called in for an interview, you've got the minimal skill set that they're looking for.

---

interview but carefully. It's a tool to help explain and illustrate but not the focus. You and your skills are the focus.

Remember that _you are going to leave the portfolio behind_ at the interview. If she wants to mark up or make notes on your portfolio, that's fine, because it's hers to keep. It's well worth it to be able to have this exchange:

Interviewer: _Now, I see here [pointing with pen] that you're...oh, wait, can I write on this?_

You: _Absolutely, I brought it for you to keep._

The best way to use your portfolio is as an illustrative tool to help show details about projects and technologies you've worked with.

Interviewer: _Have you had to maintain combined Windows and Linux networks?_

You: _Absolutely. Most of the time it's been working on existing networks, helping get them in to shape, checking for security holes, and so on. Once I had the luxury of designing a homogeneous network [flipping to "Network diagrams" in your portfolio], and I took the lessons from the previous years' work and designed this [showing the diagram to the interviewer]._

As you show your portfolio to the interviewer, keep a running checklist, on paper or in your head, of which areas you've had to show. Chances are you won't have an opportunity to show off everything in the portfolio, so you'll want to know what else you definitely want to draw attention to. If it has to wait until the end of the interview, that's OK. You can work them into your closing questions and comments.

You: *A couple items we didn't discuss in my portfolio that might be of interest are this database abstraction framework I created and some of the feedback forms I got from a training class I taught. You mentioned training problems briefly, and I thought that might interest you. I brought this copy of the portfolio to leave here.*

Wrapping up is covered in more detail in a moment.

8.6 Sell Yourself by Doing the Job

The best way to make an impression in an interview is to actually do the job that needs to be done and show that you can do it well. It's not always possible, but when you can, the payoff is huge.

Phil Morrison tells of an interview where he clearly demonstrated his expertise and landed the job.

The Whiteboard Solution
by Phil Morrison, system administrator, Milton, Florida

I'd been approached by a recruiter for a position, and the recruiter came to the interview with me. There were six people in the interview, asking me very specific questions on how I would handle merging another company's Active Directory. It was obvious that they were about to undergo such a task and did not know where to begin. I had just recently been involved in a massive AD migration and asked them whether they would like for me to draw out a possible design on the whiteboard.

I drew out how I would set up the AD along with child domains, site connectors, and so on. This brought more questions, and I answered and added more detail to the drawing, explaining why this was the best practice, positioning them for future expansion.

They asked whether I had any experience in delivering software via GPO to the desktops. I smiled and outlined the three tiers of software. I explained the concept of "thirty minutes fix or reload," the motto at my last job. I showed how they could build images that could rebuild a desktop along with all the software, detailed out roaming profiles and redirected document shares so that literally within thirty minutes they could rebuild a desktop with no data loss. I told how it could be automated so no technician would have to go onsite.

I was drawing like mad, mostly with my back to the room, adding things as the questions were asked and explaining each component. When I was done I turned and caught most of the room looking in dazed fascination at the board (all except the recruiter who was grinning like a Cheshire cat).

I asked if they had any additional questions, and they all shook their heads slowly while looking at the whiteboard, then me, and then back at the whiteboard.

They started asking me the HR-type questions, like when I could start if I was chosen. While I explained I could start tomorrow, someone noticed that the recruiter was erasing the drawings from the white board and said, "Hey, we need those!"

The recruiter answered, "No, what you need is Phil's expertise."

Afterward, we said our goodbyes, and the recruiter and I headed off to have lunch and discuss the interview. As we are buckling our seatbelts, his phone rang, and it is the client saying that they want me to start the next day.

Note how Phil demonstrated his expertise to the interviewers. He was careful to not overstep his position as a guest but rather asked if he could provide input. He demonstrated that he knew how to solve their problem, the specific problem they were facing. He clearly explained the solution to the problem in a way that everyone in the room could appreciate, if not understand.

You won't always stumble into a scenario like Phil's, with a problem begging for a solution. You'll have to make your own luck. With a little research and understanding of the company and your discussions during the interview, you can create your own scenario that lets the hiring manager see, in a concrete way, that you can do the job.

During the interview, ask about the problems that the company or the department is having, related to the job you'd like to be doing. Here are some examples:

- Are their projects behind schedule?
- Are daily server operations taking up too much time?
- Should traffic to the website be higher?

Then, turn the interview into a working meeting where you discuss the problem and your solutions for it, just like Phil did. If you can tie it back to something you've done in the past, even better. You'll be pointing at a past success.

Find out what's been tried so far to address the problem. Ask what is keeping it from being dealt with now. Is it staffing? Budget? Just popped up out of nowhere? Work these concerns into your solution.

Describe a plan for addressing the problem the hiring manager has, on a whiteboard or on paper, so that the two of you can discuss it and he can see it. That's what made Phil's story so effective. Seeing is more powerful than hearing.

Present the solution as something you are willing to take responsibility for. Make it clear that you would take care of it if given the chance. You want the manager to be able to see that hiring you would get this specific problem handled. You'd be going from someone who could do a job to someone who could fulfill a specific role in the enterprise.

For more on this technique, check out *Ask the Headhunter* [Cor97].

8.7 Closing the Interview

As you get to the end of your interview, you have three crucial steps:

1. Ask final questions.
2. Ask for the job.
3. Ask for next steps.

Ask Final Questions

The interviewer will probably ask whether you have any other questions. Go through your list, and ask those that you haven't been able to ask conversationally. If all the questions have been answered, then briefly recap what they were as go through the list to show that you did indeed bring questions with you.

You: *Let's see...we talked about the network infrastructure...talked about how I would be allowed to work on open* *source projects...reporting structure...no, that about covers it, thanks.*

Ask for the Job

Now you must ask for the job, explicitly. It may feel awkward to do this or seem like it's pushy or egotistical to come out and say, "I want this job," but you must do it. You can blow an otherwise fantastic interview by seeming indifferent to the prospect of working for the company.

You: *I wanted to thank you for the time today, and I'm very excited about the prospects. This is a job I'd like to work on I think I can bring a lot to help the project management team, and working in the sporting goods industry would be a dream for me.*

Do not shirk this all-important wrap-up step. Don't delude yourself into thinking "Of course I want the job, or else I wouldn't be here." What you see as obvious may look like indifference to the interviewer. Don't worry about being too enthusiastic by asking to move forward. Part of what you're being interviewed for is your enthusiasm and interest in the company, the department, and the team. Enthusiasm is a huge asset.

Asking for the job also tells them that even after all you've found out about the company and the job, you're still interested in moving forward. An interviewer might well think that you don't seem like you're interested, which is tragic for you if you actually are.

If you're not comfortable with the idea of expressing your interest in such a straightforward way, practice. Write a little practice sentence, and practice with someone else. Role-play it. Do whatever it takes to get you to be able to show that interest.

There is one time when it is OK to not ask for the job, and that is if you're not really interested in the job. You don't want to lie and pretend that you're more interested than you really are.

Ask About Follow-Up

Finally, ask about follow-up. Ask about what the next steps in the process are and when you can expect them to happen. It can be very simple.

You: So, what are our next steps? What timeframe are we looking at?

Interviewer: Well, we've got a another week of interviews, and then we look at them as a group, so probably the next two weeks you should hear from us.

You: That sounds fine. If I don't hear back by the 18th, may I call you? Is this number on your card best?

This part is purely for your benefit, so you may omit it if you don't really care about waiting. However, if you're like most people, after a while you'll wonder "Have they forgotten me? Are they just taking a long time?" There's no such thing as a "usual" amount of time it takes to hear back, so it's up to you to ask before you leave. This is also a good time to ask for a business card, if you haven't already been offered one, to make sure you have all the contact information you need.

Debrief Yourself

The interview process isn't over when you shake the interviewer's hand and walk out the door. You need to debrief and follow up.

After the interview, review your notes. Note important things that were said, impressions you had of people there, and what you thought you did right or wrong. Most of all, get your general impression of the job and the company so you can evaluate whether it's some place you'd want to work. You're not trying to make a decision at this point, but you want to get these facts and ideas down on paper while they're still fresh in your head. Write down everything, even if you think it's not that important. You may be surprised at how glad you are for a snippet of information a week or two down the road.

Tell someone else about your interview. It could be your spouse, a friend, or even your parents. Talking about it will bring more ideas forward, and you'll want to jot these down as well.

8.8   Phone Interviews

When you're interviewing by phone, your interviewer can't see you, so keep in mind a few techniques that will help you stand out to your interviewer.

The Phone Screen

The phone screen is a sort of mini-interview usually used to do a basic check of your skills and background before taking the time and expense of having a face-to-face interview at the company. Usually it will involve just one person from the company talking to you on the phone, one-on-one. The goal is to spend five or ten minutes up front before committing to a bigger process.

Typically, the manager or HR representative will ask a few basic questions like "You say on your résumé that you know Java. How long have you been using it?" and "Which Linux distributions are you most familiar with?" They won't be too tough, and they are usually simple statements of fact.

Even though it's called a "phone screen," don't be fooled. It's an interview, so treat it with the gravity and seriousness of a full face-to-face interview, maybe even more. One slip or one snarky comment can doom your chances of moving forward with an interview. I once called to do a phone screen and set up an interview time with a candidate who let me know how disgusted he was with his current co-workers. I never set up the interview with him.

Take the phone screen seriously. If at all possible, you should be in a quiet room away from distractions. Have someone take care of the kids, so you're not having to hiss "Shhh, Daddy's on the phone" at them.

When you're on the phone, stand. You'll project more energy than if you're sitting.

The phone screen is a great tool. It's a low-cost, low-commitment way to test the waters of compatibility. Consider it a rapid prototype of the full-blown interview.

The Telephone Interview

The telephone interview is a regular interview, but it takes place at a distance, instead of face-to-face. It is nothing like a phone screen, other than happening to be conducted over the phone.

The biggest challenge on a phone interview is that neither you nor those you'll be interviewing with can see facial expressions of the other parties involved. Seeing people's faces is a big part of listening, and without that ability everyone is at a disadvantage.

When you're having a phone interview, spend more time being explicitly clear about what you're saying. It may be useful at times to restate the speaker's words to make sure that you understand what's being said.

You: *So, to summarize, your project estimates are not very good, and you'd like those improved, but your number-one goal for this project manager position is to improve visibility and communications with upper management. Is that about right?*

Interviewer: *Yeah, that's about it.*

You: *Well, I understand the need for visibility. Management needs to know how projects are going and have quite a bit of experience in creating project dashboards....*

Avoid making jokes in any part of the interview process, because of the ease with which you can inadvertently offend or insult someone. This is especially true with the telephone interview. It's hard to tell what's a joke over the phone, and you don't want to be misinterpreted. Smileys were invented because the lack of facial expressions in email makes it hard to tell where jokes are. You don't have smileys on the phone.

Don't try to have it in a Starbucks or while you're watching the kids or in an empty conference room at your current employer on your lunch hour. Use a landline instead of a cell phone, so you don't get a dropped call. Don't have the interview at your current job, even if you have a private office.

As with the phone screen, set aside time and space. Prepare for the phone interview like you would any other interview. Assemble your materials, like a copy of your résumé to refer to. Be at a net-connected computer, but close your IM, IRC, and Twitter clients. Give the interview your full attention.

8.9   The End of Your First Day

There, that wasn't so bad, was it? Interviewing can be a chore, or it can be a joy—an exploratory look at another company or another culture. Granted, having your future employment on the line can add a bit stress, but if you keep the right perspective, it need not be so bad.

Remember, it's your first meeting with your new employer. You're there to show what a good job you can do at her company, in her department, on her problems. You want to help, and you're going to show what a good job you can do.

Now that you know how to handle the interview, move on to preparing to answer tough interview questions.

Chapter 9

Handling the Tough Interview Questions

Job interview–related threads on sites like Slashdot[1] and Reddit[2] are filled with comments from disgruntled tech workers who find stupid and offensive any question not directly related to job performance. These commenters will accuse managers of asking these tough questions only because they're in one of the aforementioned books.

Although it's possible that your questioner is a clueless robot, chances are that the questions being asked have proven to find effective answers in the past for her. Put yourself in her shoes. She has to figure out whether you are technically competent to do the job *and* if you're going to fit with the rest of the department and the company. Your technical competence is relatively easy to assess compared to how well you're going to play with others.

As you read this chapter, step back from your position as interviewee, and see these questions through the eyes of the interviewer. Try to understand how they're specifically being used so that you can aim your answer at what the interviewer really wants to know. Once you understand the purpose, answering becomes much easier.

---

1. http://slashdot.org
2. http://reddit.com

9.1 Never Give B.S. Answers

There are hundreds of books on interviewing, many specifically providing lists of "tough interview questions and the answers that will get you the job," or similar breathless claims. I've read through at least a dozen while writing this book, and I haven't seen one yet that didn't advocate giving a B.S. answer at least once.

These books all espoused reasonable principles, like never being negative and not coming across like a complainer, and I can't argue with any of that. However, when it gets down to lying, the interviewer is going to know. For example, in one book I won't name, I found this example, paraphrased:

Interviewer: *Tell me about a decision you made that your boss disagreed with.*

Bad: *When I gave notice at Yoyodyne, my boss didn't want me to leave.*

The answer is obviously B.S., even if it's factually true. It's not what the interviewer wanted to know, and you know it. It's also disrespectful, because it treats the interview like a game, where the interviewee tries to outfox the interviewer. It deliberately ignores what the interviewer is asking for. The interviewer is not going to think "Wow, if that's all they disagreed with, this guy must be good!" In fact, any good interviewer is going to say "Yes, of course he didn't, but how about another example besides that?" Curses, your memorized clever answer has been foiled!

The key to any question is to answer truthfully, from the gut, with an eye to how to help the manager and the company. Working to help the manager and the company will be your job if you're hired, and so too it is your job now. Prevarication or shading of the truth will only come back to hurt both of you.

9.2 Never Complain or Disrespect

Whatever comes out at an interview, do not gripe, and do not disrespect anyone. If you badmouth your boss, your hiring manager has to assume you'll be badmouthing her before long, too.

Even if you complain only about your current co-workers, you mark yourself as a whiner.

Gripers and whiners are toxic to a team and time-consuming to maintain. Any good manager will avoid them. Many of the questions in here are designed to dig at your tendency to complain. It doesn't matter how justified it is or if you say, "I don't like to complain about my co-workers, but...." If you're going to complain about other people, you might as well end the interview right there.

When you do answer questions that involve something negative (your greatest weakness, a project that went bad, a jerk on the team), include a follow-up explanation about how you worked to improve the situation.

9.3 Know the Red Flags the Interviewer Wants to Uncover

In addition to making sure you have the technical chops to do the work, the hiring manager wants to find out whether you're going to be a liability to hire. She's looking for warning signs that you could be a big risk. Many of the questions here try to find that out in order to give you a hole to fall into. Make sure you don't fall into the traps, and work to reassure the manager that you're not a risk.

Many of these dangers go together or are opposites of each other. As you read through this list of traits the interviewer is trying to avoid, ask yourself whether you fit either extreme.

- Candidate needs constant direction? Or cannot take direction from superiors?
- Doesn't take responsibility for actions and decisions? Or tries to take on too much responsibility or too many tasks?
- Refuses to ask for help? Or unable to work without constant hand-holding?
- Is a know-it-all? Or knows too little and is dangerous?
- Belligerent? Or wimpy?
- Blames others?
- Doesn't work on self-improvement?
- Gets bored easily?
- Uncommitted to the job?

Recognize yourself, even a little? Work on changing those negative behaviors in the long-term, but also beware of questions that seek to uncover these flaws.

9.4 The Tough Questions

The questions here are not meant to include all the tough questions you'll be asked. Indeed, the intent is to get you thinking about *how* you discuss the job and your qualifications, instead of *what* practiced speeches you can prepare.

Again, remember that the job interview is a meeting on your first day of the job. Your primary focus is what you can bring to the hiring manager and the company.

Tell Me About Yourself

This is the most important, and potentially toughest, question you'll be asked. If you're prepared for only one question, make it this one. All the other questions may or may not get asked, but this one is in every interview, even if not in these words. It's the classic opener that gives room for you to explain all the good things about you.

It's an essay question, not multiple choice. You're being asked to talk extemporaneously about who you are and what you can offer to the listener. It's an answer you must plan.

This is the worst answer, the one that says you haven't prepared at all:

Interviewer: *Tell me about yourself.*

Bad: *What do you want to know?*

This says you know nothing, or can deduce nothing, about what the interviewer is looking for in a candidate. It says that you have done nothing to think about why this job is a good fit for you. The interviewer may as well end the interview right here.

How much should you say? Talk for about thirty seconds on the high points about yourself. You want to give plenty of good starting points, without making the listener bored. You're basically putting your résumé's summary section into narrative form.

Bad: *I started out as a child...*

Bad: *I'm a programmer. Well, not now, really, because I've been out of work since January. Not much opportunity to do any programming at home. I'd really like to get this job because I don't think I have to tell you that it's hard to pay the mortgage without a paycheck, right? Oh, and my hobby is learning archaic programming languages.*

Good: *I've been a system administrator for seven years now. I started out maintaining a small ten-seat shop with one Windows NT server. Now we have a mixed Linux and Windows network with 150 users in an NT Windows domain hosted by Samba. I'm doing some programming, too, beyond shell scripting. I've written some plug-ins for the Nagios monitoring service and have contributed patches to Bugzilla. I've been working in the marketing industry for my entire career, so I think it's time to branch out. Working for Yoyodyne would be a great shift.*

Now you try it. Write down a paragraph, like the previous one, giving how you would answer the question. Use complete sentences, not just bullet points. It will be a stock answer that's not tuned for any specific job or company, but that's OK for this purpose.

No, really, go do this. Use a blank page in the back of the book if you like.

Now read it out loud. Time yourself and see how long it takes. Is it about thirty seconds in length? If it's a minute, you may be giving too much detail. If it's less than thirty seconds, chances are you're leaving out good stuff.

Do you feel comfortable reading these words? They should be fluid, and you should be comfortable with the idea of selling yourself and of talking about how good you are. Read them to a friend, and ask whether you sound normal or if you sound uncomfortable. You're not practicing lines for a play, but it is practice. You're preparing the pathways of your brain for saying these sentences.

> Practice your answers out loud to get comfortable with them.

To make it even tougher, the answer to "Tell me about yourself" is different every time. How you answer will vary depending on who you're talking to and at what stage in the interview process you're at. Consider the differences in your answer if you're in each of the following situations:

- Talking to an HR screener: Play it safe. Talk about years of experience and the different companies you've worked for. Talk about high-level qualifications (databases, Linux) over specifics (Oracle and Postgres, Red Hat and Ubuntu). Exception: Mention specific technologies listed in the ad where appropriate.

- Your future teammates: Talk nitty-gritty of technologies, throwing out relevant buzzwords to spark conversation.

- Nontechnical management: Emphasize achievements, projects, and business value provided. Keep buzzwords minimal.

- Your boss-to-be: Make it a bit of everything, with an additional emphasis on teamwork and soft skills.

Your answer may change depending on the company you're talking to and the job you're applying for. If there's an emphasis in the job ad for a specific technology, then play that up. If you have experience in the given industry, then mention that as well.

This question may come in different, more direct phrasings, such as "What makes you the best candidate for this job?" For a story of great success in answering that, see the story *Kate's Quick Reference Card* on page 129.

What Do You Know About Our Company?

This is one I like to start with, because it lets me get a sense of how prepared the candidate is for the interview. Does the candidate treat this as just another interview, or is he specifically interested in working for my company? Has he done his homework and investigated the company? For the candidate, it's should be an opening to talk about yourself in return and find out about the company's needs.

Bad: *Uh, not much, really. I thought your website was cool.*

Good: *HoseCo creates hoses and fittings for industrial applications. You've been around since 1954 and moved to this location in the 1970s. I'm interested in if you supply the aerospace* *industry? I spent a year working for Boeing's heating and cool-ing division when I was a consultant, and it was fascinating. The website uses JSP, but the online product catalog seemed to be a CGI application. Is that in Perl? You've also opened a second plant in Cincinnati, which must be a good sign for how the company is doing. What sort of communication links do you have between here and Ohio?*

From answering one question, you've shown that you are pre-pared and that you're thinking like the manager, and you've brought up part of your background that could have real bene-fit for him.

What Interests You in This Job?

All other things being equal, nobody wants to have an employee who's indifferent to the job or the company. More important, you shouldn't want to take a job that isn't interesting to you. If you can't answer this one for yourself, you shouldn't apply for the job.

Bad: *Well, it's close to my house.*

Even if it's important to work near home, that shouldn't be expressed as your primary concern. Always put the company first. This question is also the ideal place to bring up any connections you may have to the company or anyone in the company.

Good: *I've always loved cars, so working for a company that makes brake parts seems like an ideal fit. The job ad talked about using Ruby on Rails, which I've been wanting to work with. My experience has been with Java Struts. Also, my friend Susie Derkins over in Accounting says that it's a great place to work. She was telling me about how the company is very family-friendly, plus you're only about ten minutes from my house. Alto-gether, it sounds ideal.*

What Is Your Greatest Strength?

When it comes at the beginning of the interview, treat it as a focused version of "Tell me about yourself." Later in the inter-view, it's probably an attempt to assess how you see yourself. In either case, pick something that you're good at, and give examples that back it up. Better yet, pick one hard and one soft skill and play them up.

Bad: *I'm a hard worker. (So is everyone, pal.)*

Bad: *I'm a really good programmer. (This is vague, unsupported by detail.)*

Bad: *I'm like a human ASCII chart! I can tell you the hex value of any given character! (Yeah, so what?)*

Good: *I'm calm and focused in crises, and few things frustrate me. People have told me that they're amazed at how well I handle stressful situations, which you well know can happen to us system administrators in the blink of an eye.*

Good: *I have a knack for data abstraction. Creating database schemas, writing APIs...that sort of thing just comes naturally to me. It's my favorite part of the job.*

Don't worry about which strength of yours is the absolute greatest. Indeed, you'll choose the greatest strength for this company in this interview.

What Is Your Greatest Weakness?

This is the question people seem to dread most. The interviewer wants to see whether you'll say anything damning that makes you unsuitable for the job. You're not going to say anything like that, of course. Just don't let it take you by surprise, sitting in the interviewer's office pondering the question.

Most books suggest a snappy answer like "I work too hard" or "I get frustrated when people don't work as hard as I do" or "I'm a perfectionist." Those answers are good from the perspective of picking a negative and turning it into a positive, but they have two problems. First, they may not be true for you, meaning they'd be lies. Second, and worse, they are B.S., and the interviewer knows it. It has the stink of prefabricated dishonesty.

Take the question head-on. Treat it as if you'd been asked "What would you like to improve about yourself, and how are you working on it?" Be sure to make the improvement be something with you, not sound like you're blaming other people for your problems. Choose a technical weakness, not a personal failing or character flaw.

Bad: *I get frustrated when people don't work as hard as I do. (Stock B.S. answer, plus finds fault with other people.)*

Bad: *I'm a perfectionist. (Stock B.S. answer, plus what are you doing about it?)*

Bad: *I really hate testing my code. (Huge failing for a programmer.)*

Good: *I don't know enough JavaScript and Ajax. All my web programming work has been server-side, but Ajax technologies are clearly going to continue to dominate. I picked up a copy of Pragmatic Ajax the other day, and I'm working my way through it.*

Why Should We Hire You?

Assuming this question comes at the end of the interview or at the start of a second interview with a higher-up, it's your invitation to summarize yourself. Recap what you've discussed earlier in the interview, with new emphasis on what you've learned about the company's business needs and problems it needs to have solved. Give examples of specific actions you could take once on board: "You mentioned the problems your programmers were having with database normalization, and I know I could help there. Last year I led a team of DBAs who...."

Some people are intimidated by the phrasing of the question. It sounds a lot like "What's so great about you, pal?"—a challenge thrown down to the candidate. Don't think of it that way. Think of it as an aggressively worded version of "Tell me about yourself," and you'll do fine. If the question comes as a sort of opener to the interview, follow up with something like "Of course, those are only a few of the things I would bring, but I'd like to know more about the challenges your company and department face to know how I can help best."

Tell Me About a Project That Didn't Go Well

There are usually no right or wrong answers to questions like this one. The interviewer is hoping to see how you handle problems and deal with adversity. Stories are crucial here. If you get asked "Did you ever have X happen?" you treat it as "Tell me a story about how X happened."

This question works on two levels. The manager wants to see how you handle the downsides of day-to-day life and to see whether you're a blamer. Will you tell about your own short-comings or pin them on others. It's best to explain the problems on both sides of the situation, but without blaming others. Consider this standard gripe presented as an answer:

Bad: *Oh, sure, which one? The web group always has to deal with last-minute train wrecks when the marketing department comes running with some last-minute crazy project that has to be done by some dumb arbitrary deadline. Then, when they don't get what they want in the timeframe they want it, they blame us and try to make us look like chumps. It's not our fault that they can't plan ahead!*

This question is usually followed up by "What did you learn from this situation?" or "How have you changed things to prevent this in the future?"

Bad: *Not really much to learn. I guess we just have to tell the marketing department they can't have everything they want just because they want it. I'd like to give the marketing director a good book on how software projects actually work!*

Everything in these answers places the blame squarely on the shoulders of others and adds insulting language. The interviewers know that the candidate is likely to whine and malign if she comes on board. And who should improve? Not the candidate! It's the marketing director who's at fault!

Instead, consider this answer about the same situation. It describes the situation without finger-pointing or rancor.

Good: *Lately we've had some challenges with the marketing department. The new director has some aggressive plans for the website, often tied to immovable dates like trade shows. The first time we didn't get the changes in place when he wanted, there was a lot of frustration. He felt let down by the web group, and we felt like his requests were unreasonable. Clearly, there wasn't enough communication between our groups.*

Now, anticipate the follow-up without being asked for it.

Good: *After that first mess, we all got together and talked about what happened. We were glad to have the new initiative from* *marketing, but we needed to negotiate on future projects to make sure that goals were reasonable. There was resistance, but when the director saw that we were on his side, we got some real progress.*

Tell Me About the Biggest Mistake You Ever Made

This question probes at two areas. First, it addresses the handling of blame like the "project that didn't go well" question. Second, it gives a feeling of how much real experience the candidate has.

Real work means mistakes. If you're not making mistakes, you're not trying hard enough. Unless you're in an industry where mistakes are truly unacceptable, like health care or flying things, mistakes are part of life. They're also part of learning and growing in your field.

Pick a story that demonstrates that you can accept responsibility for your human mistakes. Anticipate the follow-up question "What did you learn?" in your answer.

Bad: *I dunno, I guess I don't make many.*

Bad: *I reformatted my C:\ drive once. That was pretty dumb.*

Good: *We were cutting over to a new mail system, and I was using Perl to read from Notes and write to Exchange. Monday morning, angry users found that their archive folder hierarchies had been transferred incorrectly. All messages in their archives were put in a single folder, and it was too late to rerun the conversion. From then on, I promised myself that any data conversion project had to have a post-conversion verification step before I could say it was done.*

What Would You Do If...

This is usually presented as a scenario that has no obvious good course of action to see how you handle adversity and solve problems. Even if the problem itself is technical, it's usually nontechnical judgment that you're asked about. Examples might include the following:

- While doing a company-wide software update on users' machines, you discover a folder of pornography. Of course, porn on computers is a violation of company policy. The user is fairly new to the company, and he seems like a nice enough guy. What do you do?

- You're in code freeze, two days before you're to ship a major release, and you discover a bug in a co-worker's code. You know he's had problems with his quality in the past, and he's afraid of getting a poor review. You could fix the bug easily without telling anyone, but at this point in the project, all code changes are supposed to be OKed by the project manager. What do you do?

- We're a small company, and the president of the company comes to you, furious about the website. He insists that the user registration form should use radio buttons instead of drop-down lists. He wants you to change it by the end of the day. You're technically capable of making the changes and putting them in production, but it would go against the process the department has in place. Oh, and your boss is on vacation. What do you do?

In all three cases, there's no definitively correct answer. The interviewer is probably more interested in your thought process, so make sure you explain it.

Good: *Certainly, I don't want to get the guy in trouble, and it would be easy enough to delete his porn folder and warn him that it's a violation of policy. On the other hand, policy is policy, and it's not up to me as a support tech to decide what rules to enforce. In the end, I guess I would need to... (and then explain why).*

Part of what the interviewer may be looking for is in how you dig more into the problem. Perhaps what your interviewer is looking for is for you to ask "How bad is the bug?" Go ahead and ask for more information about the situation. On the other hand, it's not a game where you ask twenty questions until you're able to derive the answer to the mystery. You must answer the question decisively.

These "What if?" questions can be a benefit for you. They're likely to be based on a real problem that the manager has had in the past. It gives you an insight to the manager, and it gives you room to follow up. After you've given your answer, ask about the question.

Good: *I'd make the president's changes, but I'd make sure I had the old versions of the code stored in version control if we needed to reverse the changes after my boss got back. It's a tough situation. Is this sort of scenario something that the department has had to deal with before?*

You're not asking what the manager thinks the right answer is, but you may very well find out. He might say, "Yeah, our VP of sales has pulled this sort of power play in the past, and everyone knows to pass the buck to me, no matter what."

Note that in the previous example, your answer differs from what the manager wants to have happen, but that's probably OK. It's your decision-making process that's being tested here, not the absolute correctness of your choice.

Questions like these can also be a test of how you would fare with the company's culture. You might find that the organization always follows the process exactly, and you think it would have been more pragmatic to give the president what he wants. That mismatch is better to find out now. Answer from the gut without waffling.

Do You Prefer to Work on Teams or Solo?

Autonomy and teamwork are two sides of the same coin. A manager has to have people on the team who can do their work without having to be led all the way. On the other hand, an employee who is unwilling or unable to work with others on a team, or cannot take direction from the manager, is often a net negative on productivity. The only bigger waste of a manager's time than hand-holding an employee is having to deal with personality conflicts between team members.

Be careful how you answer this question. Don't make it sound like you're incapable of working other than in your preferred context. As with most answers to questions like this, the answer shouldn't be simple A or B, but give examples.

Interviewer: *Do you prefer to work on teams or solo projects?*

Bad answer: *Oh, good Lord, solo projects, please.*

Almost as bad: *I find that my best work is done when unencumbered with others.*

Good answer: *Everything depends on the project. If I'm writing a one-off utility, it usually makes more sense to do it solo, maybe with a colleague's once-over to make sure I haven't missed something. Larger projects, of course, require a team, and whether tasks are done alone or in pairs depends on the nature of the task. I guess I prefer the raw speed I can usually get working solo, but most of the time, a team is what's required.*

What Do You Want to Be Doing in Five Years?

This is it—the most dreaded interview question, based on the number of people I see griping about it online and to me in person.

As much as people hate this question, the candidate's response can indicate a lot about how forward-thinking and business-minded he is. Consider this example of a short-sighted candidate.

Guess My Favorite Language!
by Adrian Howard, developer, Dorset, England

When I first started interviewing programmers, I was surprised by the folks who didn't prepare and think about the interview at all. The ones who had done no research on the company. The ones who hadn't thought about how their skills could be applied to the job. The ones who didn't seem to have a thought in their head outside of a particularly narrow technical area.

One guy stands out in my memory. When he came for his interview during the meet and greet, I asked him what books he'd been reading recently. He said he'd just picked up a book in Visual C++. Fair enough.

During the interview I asked what he saw himself doing in the role. He said "writing Visual C++ applications," even though we actually hadn't decided on an implementation language for the project. He made no mention of how this would relate to the product at all. He was worrying me a little.

Near the end of the interview I asked what he saw himself doing in five years time. He said, you guessed it, "Hopefully developing in Visual C++." Now I was scared. This person's entire focus and long-term plan was working in a single language on a single platform.

He got a polite rejection letter.

You're not getting hired just for today but for the foreseeable future. If your interviewer does *not* ask this question, or something similar, it may indicate that *he's* not interested in your long-term growth, your future at the company, or the future direction of his team. This is someone you may not want to work for.

Interviewer: *What do you want to be doing in five years?*

Bad: *I dunno.*

Bad: *Who can tell? This is the computer industry, and any answer I give you will be wrong because technology moves so quickly.*

Good: *As far as my career, I'd like to be in some sort of team lead position, but I'm not sure that management is for me. Technologically, it's hard to give specifics, of course, but my two main interests in the future are in social networking and large databases. I've always loved playing with large datasets, and the explosion of sites like Facebook I think can be transferred to business as well. Have you explored any sort of social networking here at Yoyodyne?*

There's not a right or wrong answer. If you have no interest in leadership, then don't think you have to lie and say "I'd like to be leading a team of programmers" or else be tagged a slacker. Besides, what if the interviewer isn't looking for someone to be a leader?

> Answer the question with what you know, not what you think they want to hear.

Good: *Something different from the job I'm interviewing for now, somewhere in this company. I've found that I work best as a generalist, not a specialist, and that my drive for new skills leaves me itching for new challenges every two to three years.*

Even if you have little or no work history, you still should have an eye to the future.

Good: *Since this will be my first full-time job, it's hard to know what to expect. I'd like to think that I'll have worked on a number of successful projects for the company, had a promotion or two, and learned a lot about system administration along the way.*

Most of all, be able to answer the five-year question *for yourself* before you even consider going on an interview, because if the job you're applying for doesn't fit that five-year vision, you're headed down a dead-end road.

Why Do You Want to Work for Us?

This one shouldn't even be a problem, if you've been picky about going on your interviews. You should know the answer before you ever get to the interview stage. Make sure that the primary reason you give is something about the company. After that, you can discuss what's important to you. As always, put the company first in your answers.

Bad: *I dunno, it just seemed cool.*

Weak: *I've always loved programming. (This doesn't address why this company over others.)*

Good: *Administering a network as big as you have here will be a great stretch for my skills, and I'm sure I'll learn a lot. Plus, ever since I was a little girl, I've loved airplanes, so the aerospace industry feels like a great place to work.*

Why Are You Leaving Your Job?

This can be a minefield. Be careful how you tread. You're going to be explaining why you are unhappy with a given situation, but don't complain. No matter what, do not blame others for your unhappiness.

Obviously terrible: *My boss is a jerk, and the rest of my team are a bunch of incompetent boobs.*

Just as bad: *Well, let's just say that my boss and I have differences. He's an OK guy as a person, but we just seem to clash on a lot of things. I also hate to say it, but he hasn't hired the best programmers. I love my co-workers to death, but it's frustrating to work with people who can't seem to get anything done all day.*

Soft language can't hide a griper or blamer.

The second example is softer language, but it's just as damning to you. You've explained that other people are the cause of your problems and unhappiness. You are a whiner.

Good: *I feel like I'm at the end of the road at Yoyodyne. All the projects we've been working on have been maintenance on existing systems, with nothing new. I need more challenge in my day-to-day life. I've talked to my boss, and he says that there's nothing he can do. I've learned some Ruby at home, but that's just not enough stretching for me.*

Good: *I need some place closer to home. When I started there three years ago, the hour-and-a-half commute didn't bother me. Now I find that the time on the road is such a drain on time with my family, plus it's getting more and more expensive. Of course, distance isn't the only thing that matters, but I have to say I was excited to find an opening that seemed like such a good fit here at Yoyodyne, and only fifteen minutes from home.*

Good: *My contract is up at the end of June. I looked into other openings at the company, but nothing was a fit for my skills and background.*

Good: *My salary is not at all in line with what someone with my skills and background should be making. I've checked a number of different salary surveys and compared to some cost-of-living indices. I like what I'm doing, but my boss says that the company's salary structure has no wiggle room on this. (But be prepared for the follow-up "Then why did you take the job?")*

The last example shows a case where it's safe to discuss salary, because it's in direct response to a question from the interviewer. Note that the answer doesn't take the next step and ask "So, how much is this job paying, anyway?"

In all cases, you're stating the facts without rancor or blame. In the case of a contract ending, you don't even need to make much explanation: there's just no more work.

Do You Have Any Questions for Me?

Unless you've been talking for hours, you'd better have questions to ask. See Section 7.5, *Prepare Your Questions to Ask*, on page 130 for details.

9.5 Curveballs

I was on panel of four technical managers and company vice president interviewing a candidate for the director of information technology. The candidate told us about his background as an IT director for a hospital and the achievements that he'd made during his time there. They'd installed a new phone system and PBX, upgraded server infrastructure, and overhauled the help desk. As his direct reports-to-be, we were concerned about his management style, about how he'd run the department, and so on. There were lots of fuzzy nebulous questions thrown around for an hour, and then Jerry throws out a beautiful curveball. "How many 64K channels in a T-1 line?" We were all taken aback, no one more than the candidate. We sat expectantly awaiting the answer.

To his credit, the candidate immediately came back and said, "I don't know, but I'd know who on my staff to ask for the answer." It was a good, standard answer for someone in his position, but it was a nail in his coffin.

After the interview, Jerry explained his question and why the answer was so damning. He told us "I got the sense early on that he was very hands-off, not interested in IT itself. The T-1 question should have been easy for someone who had overseen the replacement of a phone system at a hospital, but he had no idea." I laughed and said, "I didn't know the answer, and I'm no telecommunications guy, but I knew a T-1 was 1.5Mbps, and so I quickly did the math and figured it was twenty-four."

Ask for answers to questions you don't know the answer to.

Jerry confirmed my calculations. "You're right, but this guy didn't even try to figure it out. Worst of all, *the candidate didn't care.* He never asked what the answer was." We all thought about that for a bit, and our boss, the hiring manager for this position, said, "You don't always have to know technical details at a director level, but you can't be that detached, at least at this company."

There are a few lessons here. First, always ask for the answer to a technical question you don't know. I would hope that this is part of your geek nature, but if it's not, make it part of how you live. It will help you for the rest of your career, not just interviewing.

Second, interviews are as much about fit as technical know-how. You can argue whether an IT director needs to know the nitty-gritty of how things work under his command or whether it's best to be hands-off, but that doesn't matter in this case. What we discovered throughout the interview was that he was not right for the company. Your interviews will be about fit as well, even with the hard technical questions.

Third, never forget the vast difference between what you mean to say, the words you actually say, and what those words tell the listener.

9.6 More Tough Questions: Exercises for the Reader

Now that I've shown some examples of tough questions, and how to answer them to let the hiring manager know what she wants to know, I'll leave the following as food for thought. All of these are good examples of questions that managers use to dig into how a candidate will handle conflict and adversity and to assess cultural fit:

- Tell me about a time your work was criticized unfairly.

- What is something you've disagreed with your boss about?

- How do you deal with people you don't like?

- What did you like best about your last job? Least?

- How do you handle pressure?

- How long have you been looking? How's the job search going? What's the market like out there?

- How are you going to like working at a little company like ours, after spending years at MegaCorp?

- Tell me about a team member you just couldn't get along with.

- Tell me what you think of your boss. How do you and your boss get along?

- What during the workday motivates you? What demotivates you?

- What's an example of something you don't like about your current job? What would you do to change it?

Answer each question, perhaps on paper, and look back at it from the perspective of the interviewer. Does it show you in your best light? How else might an interviewer interpret your answer? Can you reduce the chances of your answer being misinterpreted?

Job interviewing isn't easy, but these exercises should help give you the mental practice to do your best.

Chapter 10

Too Much Information

Imagine yourself in a job interview, where you're just making introductions. The interviewer explains a bit about the company and asks the classic opener, "So, tell me about yourself." Trying to give the interviewer an idea of what a determined, hard worker you are, you open with this:

> After my wife and I arrived here in Ohio from Germany at age 35, I trained my son to play piano. He even performed at our church.

Your intent was to show that you're a committed family man with strong roots in your heritage, that you have the skills to raise a child, and that you're active in your church community, right? In fact, the result of your little bit of exposition probably will be to make the interviewer very nervous. It may even exclude you from a job. That one little sentence covered five bits of information an employer can't ask you, because it's illegal in the United States to discriminate based on (among other things) marital status, country of origin, age, family, or religious affiliations.

In all communications with the company, whether in person, in email, or on paper, keep things professional and factual. Anything else is TMI: Too Much Information.

10.1 Illegal Topics

In the United States, discrimination laws are specific. A number of factors relating to an employee or potential employee cannot be used as the basis for discrimination. For example, an employer may not decide against hiring a candidate because the candidate practices a certain religion, is from a certain country, has children, or is of a certain age. Every employer is aware of these laws, and the vast majority are careful to make sure that not only are no decisions made that break the law but also to avoid even the possibility that someone could think an illegal hiring decision was made. No employer wants to invite a lawsuit.

Just as the company must not bring up any discussion of these forbidden topics, do not discuss them yourself. You may not have any nefarious reasons for bringing them up, but the interviewer may rightly wonder "Why is this guy telling me he's Hispanic? Is he trying to put us in a situation where he can claim discrimination if we don't hire him?" The rule to follow is this: "If it's not legal for the company to ask you about a given piece of information, don't volunteer it."

The following are most of the classes for which it is illegal to discriminate based on in the United States.

Race and Ethnic Background

We'd be horrified if an interviewer asked something as brazen as this:

Bad Interviewer: *Were either of your parents Hispanic?*

But what if my friend Pete Krawczyk went to an interview and was asked this:

Bad Interviewer: *Krawczyk...is that Polish?*

Was the interviewer making small talk, or was he trying to determine that Pete was Polish and therefore an unfit candidate? I would hope the former, but it doesn't really matter: it's not a topic for discussion.

Even if you feel like your ethnic background is incredibly obvious, because your name is Gloria O'Connell or Yaakov Sloman or Kevin Falcone or Ricardo Julian Besteiro Signes, or you think "Of course anyone can tell that I'm black," it's not a topic for discussion.

Not all cultural discussions are forbidden. Feel free to discuss areas of travel and study of other countries and cultures, as long as your personal background does not enter into it.

Good: *I spent a year studying architecture in Naples and Rome. There's a beauty being there that you can't get out of pictures.*

TMI: *I spent a year studying architecture in Naples and Rome. I really felt connected to my ancestors.*

Sometimes a job qualification, or something you bring to the position, will dance dangerously close to a forbidden topic. Discuss legitimate topics, but be careful.

Good: *I understand the company is working a lot with clients in Mexico. I speak fluent Spanish.*

TMI: *I grew up with Spanish as my first language.*

Religious Affiliations

Not only are your religious beliefs a protected class under U.S. law, but they're also a hot topic that may sway a potential employer against you. Even if you feel you're part of the mainstream, such as if you're a Christian in the United States, any discussion of your religious beliefs is inappropriate and will probably work against you.

The only case when your religious background is appropriate for discussion is when it may have an effect on your ability to do the job. For example, I interviewed a candidate whose Jewish faith required he be home each Friday before sundown to observe the Sabbath. He handled the situation beautifully. He waited until the end of our interview to bring it up, since there was no reason to bring up a potential negative early on in the interview. We discussed it frankly and respectfully. He explained that he would probably need to leave by 5 p.m. on Fridays in the summer and 2 p.m. in the winter if he was to be home before sundown and would then be unavailable to work until Sunday. Most important, he assured me that he would work as necessary to make up the time the rest of the week. At no point did we discuss the religious aspects of his needs, only that they were there and whether the working requirements of the position could accommodate them.

Consider what obligations you may have that may fall outside the mainstream of U.S. legal holidays. Do you need off for Passover and other Jewish holidays? Need prayer times during the day? These all affect your work throughout the day and should be discussed honestly. If it's possible, leave out the details of why, and stick only to the work details:

Interviewer: *Sometimes we have projects that require weekend work. Do you have anything that would affect your availability?*

Good answer: *I have personal obligations on most Sunday mornings.*

TMI answer: *I teach Sunday school most Sunday mornings over at Holy Apostles.*

Family, Children, and Pregnancy

Family is one of those topics that is hard to avoid if there's any discussion of your nonwork life, but it's also potentially the most damaging in the eyes of an unenlightened interviewer.

An interviewer might fear that a parent of five children will need to take off more time from work than someone with no children or that a married candidate won't be able to burn the midnight oil as much as one who is unmarried. Maybe there's a fear that a pregnant woman will need too much maternity leave or that co-workers won't want to work with a pregnant woman. These are not legitimate reasons for discrimination under U.S. hiring law.

Avoid bringing up family.   I'm not suggesting that you remove all traces of your family. You don't need to remove your wedding ring before an interview. Still, avoid bringing up family if you can, and be wary of an interviewer who asks.

Age

Your age is a factor that has no bearing on your abilities and so is illegal to ask about. Be sure to leave out any mentions of facts that might peg your age at a given number. When listing your college experience, list only degrees attained or coursework completed, but without mention of years. If for some reason high school is discussed or is required on an application, give only the name and city of the school, not the years you attended.

Health and Physical Factors

In tech jobs, your physical health usually doesn't enter into the job requirements. The exceptions may be for tech support or sysadmin positions with certain physical requirements, like being able to string cable or lift equipment up to fifty pounds.

If you have certain health accommodations that would need to be made, then it makes sense, later in the interview process, to ask what sort of physical requirements there may be. If there are health issues that would prevent you from performing one of the duties, or that would affect your day-to-day work, discuss only the effects on the job, not the cause.

Interviewer: *Sometimes we have to work late. Is there anything that would affect your availability?*

TMI answer: *I have dialysis therapy every Tuesday and Thursday at 5 p.m.*

Good answer: *I have personal obligations on Tuesday and Thursday evenings, but beyond that, I don't see any conflicts.*

Any Other Illegal Topic

I've only skimmed the biggest no-nos of what can't be discussed in the hiring process. These are guidelines to keep in mind and are certainly not authoritative. To find out more, visit the U.S. Equal Employment Opportunity Commission's website[1] or your local public library for state-specific details.

10.2 Other Topics to Avoid

It's not just the illegal topics that should be left out of the job-hunting process. Here are some other areas of discussion that should be avoided. It's not just the hot-button topics you'd expect, either.

Your Financial Information

Many companies will ask for your salary history to try to figure out how little they need to pay you or to decide whether you're "overqualified" for the job. Do not tell them. For more about why to keep your salary history to yourself and how to do so politely, see Section 6.4, *Never Tell Anyone Your Salary History*, on page 116.

---

1. http://www.eeoc.gov

Sexual Orientation

Although sexual orientation is not a federally protected class when it comes to employment opportunity, some states or localities may have their own laws protecting discrimination based on sexual orientation. Legal issues aside, any discussion of sex or sexuality is inappropriate. It's also one of the easiest ways to offend a potential employer.

Politics

Politics is the other old standby, along with sex, of what to never discuss at the office. Republican? Democrat? Vote 'em all out regardless? Discuss it outside of work.

The exception to the politics rule is if it applies directly to your professional background. For example, my friend Tom Limoncelli[2] believed strongly in Howard Dean's presidential bid in the 2004 campaign. He believed in it so much that he worked as a system administrator for the campaign for nine months in 2004. Certainly, this is a valid item for Tom to put on his résumé. That said, I would hope that Tom would keep discussion of this work background in an interview strictly to the work aspects of this part of his employment history.

On the flip side, another friend, Dave Rolsky, works with a number of animal rights organizations and doesn't mention any of them during the job-hunting process. However, he does list on his résumé his work for a vegetarian restaurant search engine, because it demonstrates his skills as a web programmer.

You may think "Why keep it a secret, if it shows up in my Google footprint anyway?" It's not that you're keeping your life a secret, or hiding it, but rather that you're not bringing up potential distractions. If in doubt, keep things strictly business.

Clubs and Organizations

Sometimes you may feel like giving a little more background about who you are outside of work, but this sort of information may influence someone against you and probably won't help you anyway.

---

2. Tom's *Time Management for System Administrators* [Lim06] is a great book for everyone who has too much to do and not enough time to do it.

Clubs and organizations often have political overtones. Maybe you enjoy skeet shooting, which might make someone think you're a member of the NRA and a staunch defender of the absolute freedoms of the Second Amendment. Perhaps you also play in a Megadeth cover band or sing in a community choir, which may give someone the impression that you're a drug-addled burnout or a religious zealot. All of these have potential of tipping someone's opinion against you, so unless they apply directly to your professional background, don't discuss them.

With all of these topics, it can be a judgment call as to where it's appropriate to bend these rules. Maybe you think your experience in community theater helps your work as a project manager. As always, use your own judgment over what anyone else says, even this book.

10.3 Handle Inappropriate Questions Tactfully

Chances are that somewhere in your job hunting someone is going to ask you an illegal, or at least inappropriate, question. Johanna Rothman has heard some doozies.

"Are You Pregnant?"

by Johanna Rothman, speaker/author/consultant, Boston, Massachusetts

I was looking for a job in the months after I was married, and I was astonished at the comments. "Wow, what a rock," said, one interviewer. "Thank you, my husband has great taste." One HR person looked at my engagement ring, which is really not that big, and said "You don't need to work, do you?" "Sure I do," told her, "I'm keeping him, not the other way around."

At one interview, the hiring manager asked, "Are you pregnant?" I was floored and said, "No. Why do you ask? Is my stomach fat?" The hiring manager said, "Oh, you can't catch me with that one; that's like the 'Are my hips too big in this dress?' question from my wife." I laughed so hard I thought I would lose it. Then I said, "Gotcha. Now you owe me big, because you just turned this into a sex discrimination case." He literally paled, and I pealed off into laughter again. I'm pregnant just because I got married? Please. One does not cause the other.

As satisfying as I'm sure it was for Johanna to put the guy in his place, I'd suggest a more low-key response should you ever be in a similar situation. Johanna later added, "Humor in person can work to defuse potential discriminatory situations. But, don't use humor early in the interview before you've built rapport."

Give the interviewer the benefit of the doubt, that it was an honest mistake, not an attempt to find out information to use against you. An interviewer idly saying "Krawczyk...is that Polish?" probably meant it as friendly small talk, especially if he's doing his best to pronounce it correctly.

> **Give the interviewer the benefit of the doubt.**

You want to handle the situation gracefully. There's nothing to be gained by putting the interviewer on the defensive. You also don't want to weaken your position by answering the inappropriate question. Since you're going off the assumption that the interviewer made an honest mistake, there's no need to be defensive.

Answer the question with another question:

Interviewer: *I'm glad to meet you, Amanda. My daughter's name is Amanda, too. Got any kids yourself?*

You, without venom or sarcasm: *With so much to talk about this afternoon, I'd rather talk about the job and my qualifications. I did notice what looked like some workers stringing cable. Are you expanding bandwidth for the building?*

Do not use a sarcastic tone. You don't want to be aggressive or make the interviewer feel stupid. If he realizes his error, he'll be embarrassed enough as it is. Note how by side-stepping to another topic, you've left the interviewer a way to move forward and leave his gaffe behind. You've also turned it to your positive by showing that you're paying attention. Little details like this are a great way to move conversations forward and show your interest in the company.

10.4 Who Wants to Work for a Company Like That Anyway?

You may be thinking "If a company is clueless enough to not know about Equal Employment Opportunity laws, or an interviewer really thinks he's entitled to know my marital status, would I really want to work for them anyway?"

It's a fair question, but the time to ask it is after you have a job offer, not in the middle of an interview. The goal of an interview is to get a job offer or to move on to the next phase of the hiring process. You have nothing to lose by going ahead with an interviewer who makes mistakes like these, but everything to gain by leaving your options open.

10.5 It's All About Focus

While all this talk about illegal and inappropriate questions may be intimidating, the point is not to worry about what not to say but to maintain focus on what really matters. You're sending in your résumé, or participating in an interview, to show the hiring manager that you can do the work that needs to be done and that you can do it well. Anything else may well be too much information.

Chapter 11

After the Interview: The Job Offer and Beyond

The interview is out of the way, but what next? It could be just about anything: a quick job offer, more interviews, or weeks of agonizing waiting. Maybe it will be more interviews followed by weeks of agonizing waiting.

This part of the employment process can be the toughest to play. Rejection is a likely outcome of your interaction with the company, but it need not be the end of your chances at employment there. You may get a job offer, but it may not be one you want to accept without careful research and negotiations. How you handle these interactions with the company can affect whether you get the job and how you're perceived once the job starts. Most important, how you handle leaving your old company can have effects, both positive and negative, on your career and future job prospects years down the road.

11.1 Send Thank-You Notes

The day of the interview, or the day after at most, send a thank-you note to the hiring manager. You want to thank her for her time and her interest and express again your interest in the job. It doesn't have to be fancy or long.

For example:

> Dear Mr. Manager,
>
> Thank you for the opportunity to meet with you today. I enjoyed the interview and tour and discussing your database administration needs. I'm even more confident after our discussion with Peter Programmer that I would be a valuable addition to the Yoyodyne team. I look forward to hearing from you.
>
> Sincerely,
> Susan Candidate.

Write this note on a simple note card, not in email. You can get a box of note cards at any drugstore for a buck or two. Address it to the manager at the company. The physical note card will help keep you in the mind of the manager and will help you stand out from the rest of the candidates who have interviewed with the manager. If you've met other significant people at the interview, such as being part of a panel interview, then go ahead and send thank-you notes to all of them.

Thank-you notes are an opportunity.

Sometimes people will ask "Do I have to send a thank-you note to so-and-so?" but that's the wrong attitude. Turn that around into "Do I get to send a thank-you note to so-and-so and provide another opportunity to make a good impression on him or her?" Always be selling yourself.

11.2 And Now You Wait...

You've had the interview, you think it went well, but now what? "When can I expect to hear back," I hear you asking. "How long should it take? What's average to get a response from an interview? It has been a week...is that a good sign or bad? For the love of God, Andy, *soothe my frantic worries with clear answers!*" I'm sorry, Gentle Reader, but I can't.

There's no such thing as "average." I once had a job offer before I got home from the interview. Sometimes you'll never hear back. The sad truth is that you're going to have to wait for a while, and it probably will be more than you want. Double that amount of time for waiting if you're job hunting in late November or December when people go on vacation and corporate wheels turn slowly.

Consider the amount of calendar time that can pass. If the position you're applying for is open to the world and the hiring manager has dozens or hundreds of résumés, chances are she's interviewing at least three or four likely candidates. Those interviews don't come easy, since schedules have to be arranged. It will likely be days, if not weeks, before all the interviewing can be done.

There are two ways to know when you can expect to hear back: ask at the interview, or ask after the fact. Asking at the interview, as discussed in Section 8.7, *Ask About Follow-Up*, on page 158, is the least stressful way to do it, and it shows that you're forward-thinking.

If you're past that stage and you haven't heard back but are you're wondering when you will, you can contact the hiring manager or the HR department, depending on who drove the interview. There are three ways you may make this contact safely:

- Call the hiring manager, speak to her, and ask her.
- Call the hiring manager, get her voicemail, and ask her.
- Email the hiring manager and ask her.

Those are your three choices, and they are mutually exclusive. Do not, for example, leave a voicemail *and* send email, because that crosses from "legitimate question" into "annoying and pushy."

Regardless of the form of communication, you need to express your desire to move forward, offer to help in any way, and ask for some kind of timeline when you could expect to hear back. Refer to Section 8.7, *Ask About Follow-Up*, on page 158 for an example.

The only question is "How long should I wait?" I'd suggest waiting at least a week, before you get too impatient. The best solution, of course, is to ask before you leave the interview.

Waiting doesn't mean that you're not still working on your job search, however. You can still be looking for other opportunities, further researching the company in preparation for a second interview, or investigating salary norms for the industry and location of the company, in preparation for a job offer.

11.3 Go for Further Interviews

A second interview is a great sign. It means you've passed the initial technical screening. The hiring manager is interested enough to spend more time taking a look at you. Typically the first interview is with just one or two people, and the second interview (and third and fourth...) will be with more and from a broader circle. Whereas the first interview probably centered on technical skills, the second will probably be more about team fit and you as person.

The rules for interviews after the first are the same as before, but the interview will probably be tougher on you. You'll have to meet more people, and it may well be frustrating answering the same questions as before. Don't look at these repeated questions as annoyances. Instead, see them as more opportunities to sell yourself on how great you are for the position. Every time you're asked "So what did you do at your last company," it's your time to shine. You can tailor your answers to the audience as well. The way you answer about your last job should probably be different when you're telling a fellow system administrator than when you're telling your boss-to-be and different from when you're telling the vice president.

The interview with the president or vice president is a curious custom. I've seen many situations where everyone to be hired must have an interview, even if only for five or ten minutes, with someone from upper management, typically the vice president of IT or, if the company is small enough, the president. Although meeting with someone that high in the company hierarchy can be intimidating, don't worry. Typically, the executive will impress upon you the importance of your position and your department on the future of the company, and you'll get tossed a few simple questions. Unless you do something like insult his mother, you'll be fine.

Even with the likely emphasis on team fit and personality, prepare for the subsequent interviews with the same diligence you applied to the first. Bring whatever you brought to the first to the second. Your meetings with the new people are first interviews to them.

11.4 Give Solid References

At some point before you get a job offer, you'll probably be asked for a list of employment references. You don't have to have a special format where it looks nice like a résumé. Emailing the hiring manager or HR department is probably all you need to do. Don't be surprised by this important part of the job hunt. Your references could be the deciding factor in whether you land a job.

Typically, your references will get checked after you've had an interview or two and the hiring manager is ready to give you a job offer or is narrowing down candidates. Reference checks are very time-consuming in terms of calendar time, since the people involved may not be available for days, so they'll be saved until last. There are two ways to check references: the HR way and the hiring manager way. Either or both may be used on you.

The HR way is to call up past employers to verify your past employment, that you worked the time you said you did, and that you had the title you claimed. It's entirely factual and free of judgment. This kind of checking is easy in the United States, because it's unlikely to cause any problems.

The hiring manager way is more typically used for higher-level positions and is about judgment about your capabilities. In the United States, some employers are wary of giving out this type of information for fear of lawsuits. Some companies may forbid managers from giving references and require that all requests for references be sent to the HR department. This type of reference is what I'll be talking about in this chapter.

The questions a hiring manager will ask your references are likely to be the same questions he asked you at the interview, but asking a third party. "What was Bob like to work with?" and "What was Bob's greatest strength?" and "Did he do better with teams or alone?" are all questions you've likely heard at the interview, and your references will probably will hear them as well.

Unfortunately, reference checking is often the slowest part of the hiring process and can be the most frustrating for both the hiring manager and the candidate. Many times I've been eager to talk to some references about a candidate I was considering hiring but had to wait days to get in contact with the references or to schedule time when the two of us could talk.

Who Should I Use as a Reference?

The best reference you could possibly have would be your most recent manager, who has had to lay you off because of circumstances beyond his control. He'll lament your departure and will sing your praises because he wishes that he could continue to have you on the staff. He'll emphatically declare that if he could hire you back, he would. That's usually not possible, so who's next?

Barring the ideal case already mentioned, who should you refer your future boss to for confirmation of everything you've discussed in the interview? Consider the questions that will be asked of your reference. Start with the ideal reference and work backwards from there. A former boss, former co-workers, and even current co-workers are your main pool to choose from. Think of people who can attest to the work you've done in the past. If possible, include people you've reported to, people who have been your peers, and, if possible, people who have reported to you. This could include members of teams you've been the lead on.

 Do not use relatives as references. These are business references, not personal references like you might put on a college application. Unless you worked directly for or with the relative in question, they will not be able to supply the information the hiring manager is looking for. Even then, a relative's assessment of your work is likely to be dismissed as being prejudiced, and you'll probably look foolish listing your uncle on a reference sheet. Best to ignore the relative altogether.

Being a friend of yours is not enough to be a reference either, unless your friend is someone you've worked with and can discuss your work. In fact, considering that many of the friends we make in life are people we've worked with or for, it would be difficult to get a list of references that didn't include at least one person we would call a friend.

The references you present to a company that asks for references may change depending on the type of job you're applying for. If I were applying for a programming or managerial job, I'd list my current boss and co-workers. However, if I were to apply for a job as a programming instructor, I'd include the conference chairs of the conferences I've spoken at over the past decade. As with everything, there's no one-size-fits-all answer.

Acting as a reference is a big responsibility, and you want to make sure that whoever you ask is someone who will represent you well. Consider how this person is going to sound on the phone or in email to the person from your new company who calls to ask about you. If you wouldn't be proud to introduce someone at the new company to your potential reference, you probably want to rethink your choice.

> Consider how your reference will represent you to the company.

If your colleague agrees to be a reference, thank her profusely, and discuss what she might want to talk to a company about. "Remember that GUI enhancement project we worked on a few years ago? How well that went, even though the requirements from marketing kept changing every week? I think that would be a good thing to bring up if possible." In a way, a reference check is a mini-interview, and you want to help your colleague be as prepared as possible.

If you're working in open source or other community projects, don't overlook the potential of references from there. Although probably not as valuable as the endorsement of a boss or co-worker, the projects you've worked on outside of your normal 9-to-5 job are still valuable work experience.

How to Create a Reference Sheet

Creating a list of references doesn't require any creativity or special formatting. Just give the facts that the reference checker will need to make an effective reference check. For each reference, you'll need to list at least the following:

- Full name

- Position and current company
- Email address(es)
- Phone number(s)
- How you know the person and what work you've done together

Here's a sample of what you might do:

```
Maggie Majercik
Director of Internet Operations
ExampleCom, Inc.
Work: 815-555-8324
Cell: 608-555-9431
maggie@example.com

Maggie was my boss from 2005 to 2008 before she left Yoyodyne.
She is currently working for ExampleCom.


Ronald Barker
Database Administrator
Yoyodyne
Cell: 414-555-2173
rbarker@localisp.com

Ron is a member of my department at Yoyodyne.  We've worked together
on various projects since 2006.

Email will be the best contact method for Ronald.
```

Note how you've provided everything that the reference checker might need to know to do the reference check and have given some background. In Maggie's case, that she has a director-level position should lend some weight to her words about you, so she should be your top reference. In the case of Ronald, you've given only his home contact information, because you don't want your employer-to-be to be calling your current workplace to get references. The hiring manager will respect and understand this, so just spell it out explicitly.

Whatever information you put on the sheet for the person acting as a reference, make sure that person verifies it first.

Before You Hand Over Your Reference Sheet

Do make sure that you let your references know that they may get called. Do this every time you provide them as references, just to make sure that they're not surprised to get a call or email. It also helps ensure that your reference isn't unavailable for some reason. You also can help your reference know what to expect. Your communication can be as simple as an email:

You, in email: *Hey, Bob, things are going well with my talks with Yoyodyne. I've gone through three interviews, and they just asked for references, so I gave them your name. The manager, Sarah, has had some team issues, so she may ask a lot about team fit. I told her that since you and I had been on so many teams together, you'd be an ideal contact. As always, thanks for helping me out in my search.*

That email is short, simple, and crucial. It gives Bob a heads-up that he may get a call. It gives him background on what to expect. Most of all, it shows your appreciation to Bob for performing this crucial role. You don't want to neglect your references and have them unwilling to perform this valuable service. Good references are gold, so maintain them.

Make sure that your references have actually received the email and are available. Ask for an acknowledgment. If your reference is spending two weeks in Europe and not checking email, you'll want to use someone else, so the manager who wants to hire you isn't sitting waiting to contact your reference.

11.5 The Job Offer

When the job offer comes in, you'll be excited. It might be by email or a phone call, or they might call you back in to the office to make the offer in person. No matter how the offer is made, there's only one way to respond to a job offer.

You, even though you're excited: *Thanks very much, I'm glad we're at this stage. Of course, I'll need some time to examine the offer. When would be a good time to talk to you tomorrow?*

You thank the hiring manager or HR representative graciously, express your happiness at having moved forward, and then you *do not accept the position yet.* I don't care if the money's good and it's a great place to work and your rent is due in a week—do not accept on the spot. The job offer can wait twelve to twenty-four hours.

You need time to evaluate the offer in its entirety. Of course, you wouldn't have gone this far if you didn't want the job, but it's time to make your final moves. The decision to take a position is a big one and shouldn't be taken lightly. For those with spouses or other family to contend with, the need for reflection is even greater.

Don't worry about the company needing an answer right away. Any reasonable manager will understand wanting to wait a day or two. He'll probably ask for some kind of deadline ("So, can I hear back from you by Thursday noon?"), which is certainly reasonable to not want to be left hanging. If you do get pressured to take the position immediately, look at it as a red flag that may point to something more troubling.

What to Ask About

Now that you have the job offer, the rule of "Everything is about the company" is reversed. Now is the time to ask all the details and specifics that you want to know. Examples may include the following:

- What are the expected work hours? Is there a set minimum of hours you must work?
- What are the details of the benefits? Tuition reimbursement? Matching charity donations? Any perks like a company laptop?
- Are there expected days you must work or travel you must take? Maybe a yearly trade show everyone goes to?
- What's the dress code like?

Most of these questions are likely answered in the company's employee manual, if it has one. Ask to see it. Take home a copy if they'll let you. This will give you excellent insight into the culture of the company and what's expected.

There's nothing wrong with making sure you have answers to all your questions. Assume nothing. If, for example, dress code matters to you, don't assume that you can dress the way you saw everyone, because it might have been Hawaiian shirt day and everyone is normally in a suit and tie. The time to ask is before you start the job.

Check the health benefits very carefully, assuming the company offers them. Ask to see the specifics of the health coverage. The HR department should be able to give you details. The health coverage is part of the total compensation you earn and should be factored into the total dollar value of the job. If you go to another company for a salary increase of $5,000 per year but their prescription drug coverage doesn't cover your maintenance medications and you wind up paying $250 per month out of pocket, it's really only a $2,000 increase.

Consider your future needs as well. If you and your spouse have been trying in vain to have a child and have considered fertility treatments, an insurance policy that covers fertility treatments could be worth tens of thousands of dollars.

Negotiate the Offer

The best way to negotiate salary is not to negotiate. Negotiating salary starts out both parties to be at odds with each other.

Say you get an offer for $60,000 per year. Ask yourself, "Is that enough for me to take this job?" The question shouldn't be "Could they be paying me more?"

First, the entire back and forth of negotiating a salary is at its core a competitive one. You're trying to get more from them; they're trying to get more from you. It starts out the relationship on a combative stance.

Second, the company is foolish to try to underpay you. It's just not in its best interests long term. Say that you're going to be doing a job worth $60,000 to the company, and that's an appropriate salary for that geographic area. If they offer to pay you $55,000 for the job and you accept, then you're underpaid. You're going to know that you're underpaid, if not at first, then when you sniff around. You're going to look for a higher-paying job, where you'll be paid the $60,000 you're worth, and you're going to be unhappy with the company. Eventually, you'll quit, and the company has to go through the hiring process again.

I hear some of you asking "But what if the people at the company aren't that smart?" Then it sounds to me like it's not a company you want to work for—a company that would save a few thousand dollars a year and risk throwing away its investment.

Once you have an offer and you've spent a day thinking about it, you have three choice: make a counteroffer, decline the offer, or accept the offer.

Make a Counteroffer

If the offer tendered isn't what you need, usually because the pay is too low or there are work requirements that won't work for you, then you turn down the offer and explain what your requirements are. It can't hurt to ask, if your request is reasonable.

Salary too low: *I appreciate the offer. I'd love to work for Yoyodune, but to make this move, I'd need to be at least at $67,000. Is there something you can do to help make this work out?*

Not enough vacation: *I'm afraid that I'm not going to be able to make this move with the offer as presented. I'd love to work at Yoyodyne, but one week of vacation isn't going to work for me. Can we do something to make this work for both of us?*

Note how you've stated the problem clearly and anticipated the follow-up question of "What do you need?" This puts the ball back in their court. You may get an answer of "I'm sorry to hear that; that's the best we can do," or you may hear "Let me go back to HR and see whether there's any wiggle room on the vacation policy."

> **Your reasons for your requirements are yours alone.**

Please do not imagine that you are obligated to account for your requests. You do not need to, and indeed should not, explain your logic for your salary or other requirements. Explaining the logic behind these requirements leaves open the door for negotiation, and they're not open for negotiation. Maybe you've got a kid who needs a new pancreas, you've got an expensive mistress, or maybe you just like to roll around in cash like Scrooge McDuck. Your requirements are your requirements, and if you're comfortable with them, they must be as well.

Decline the Offer

Sometimes you just have to say "Thanks, but no thanks." Maybe the compensation isn't what you need, and the difference in pay is one that you're sure won't be surmountable and you don't want to look greedy. Perhaps you've uncovered parts of their culture or the job duties that have helped change your mind about wanting to work there. Your need only decline the offer, not unlike the counteroffer, but without leading to what might make it possible. Give some indication of why, but no specifics.

Salary too low: *I appreciate the offer. I'm afraid that I'm going to have to turn it down. The salary is just not where I need it to be.*

Insufficient benefits: *I'm afraid I'm going to have to turn this job down, as much as I would love to be part of Yoyodyne. The benefits package isn't what I've become accustomed to.*

If you're asked specifics, you need only repeat the basic complaint or a slight variation: "It's just not where I needed; we have a pretty big difference between the offer and my requirement." Make sure that you're not casting aspersions on the company by saying anything like "You guys don't pay very much." You're just describing a difference, not finding fault.

If there are other, less quantifiable issues, they should be described as well, but remember to keep it as description, not accusations. Again, you need not spell out specifics.

Good: *I'm afraid I'm going to have to decline. I've thought about where I'm going in my career and reexamined all that I've learned about Yoyodyne over the past few days, and I just don't see us as a long-term match.*

Bad: *I'm afraid that if I come on board here I'm going to wind up doing 90 percent grunt sysadmin work and little to no programming.*

Good: *I've met quite a few great people here at Yoyodyne, but I'm afraid I wouldn't fit in well here. I'm going to need to find a team that's a better match.*

Bad: *Half your programmers turned out to be real jerks, and you, as boss, seem to have done nothing about it.*

If the problem is with culture or the job, for example, be prepared for the reasonable question, "Why did you let things get to the point of an offer?" If you know a company isn't a fit, let them know. It's only fair.

Accept the Offer

If the offer is to your liking, then go ahead and accept. No need to dance around what you didn't like. However, you'll probably need to negotiate your starting date. Although it's custom to give your old employer two weeks' notice before leaving, there's no law that I'm aware of that mandates that. Since you don't want to burn any bridges and you want to be well-remembered, that two-week buffer is one that makes sense. If that works out with your new employer, then so be it. If they want you to start sooner, you need to balance the needs of your new employer with your need to keep in your old employer's good graces.

> Always get an offer in writing before taking action.

Never accept an offer without seeing a written offer. Never give notice at your old employer without the written offer in hand. Verbal offers can easily be rescinded. Get an offer letter from them that spells out, at the very least, your annual salary, your benefits package, any additional perks, and your starting date. Make sure the printed letter matches your expectations. This isn't a matter of trust or mistrust but of making sure there are no misunderstandings. If you're at all unsure of something, ask. Maybe you get a week of vacation the first year, but is that first calendar year or first year of employment? Oh, first *fiscal* year? Good thing you asked!

Make sure the offer is from the HR department or an officer of the company, not just an email from the hiring manager. It would be tragic to find that you'd resigned your old position, only to find that the hiring manager at your new company didn't have the authority to extend the offer to you and, oh, so sorry, that offer isn't valid.

Until you have the offer in writing, don't breathe a word to anyone that you've accepted the job, because until you have the offer, you really haven't. Don't tell your buddy at the next cube over, and certainly don't start packing up your cube thinking no one will notice. You have clearance from me to tell your spouse and your mom if you have to. That's it.

When you finally have a written offer, it's time to resign.

11.6 Leave Your Job Gracefully

Leaving a job isn't just a matter of telling your boss you quit. It's a stressful action for all involved, both you and your boss. Handle it carefully just as you'd handle any other business situation. Your actions here can give you a terrible reputation or can make friends for a lifetime.

Write a simple, brief resignation letter. As always, include no judgments and include only the absolutely necessary facts.

> October 31, 2009
>
> Dear Arthur Carlson,
>
> I will be resigning my position as System Administrator II for Cincinnati Radio Holdings. My last day will be November 14, 2009.

Don't explain your departure. Date the letter, print it, and sign it. Present it to your boss. Congratulations, you've just resigned.

Now that you've resigned, there's no going back. I hope you got the new job offer in writing.

Decline Any Counteroffer

Your current employer may try to entice you to stay, usually by offering you a raise. Don't take it. Taking a counteroffer is about as bad a career move as you can make.

First, before your resignation from Company A, you accepted an offer from Company B to go work for them. To accept a counteroffer from Company A means you must go back on your promise to Company B. Imagine if you'd had an offer rescinded on you. That's how Company B will see you.

Second, your time at Company A will probably be short-lived. You've just told your boss that you want to leave, that you're itching to go, and that you can be bought off with a salary bump. You can bet that they'll be looking for replacements as soon as possible.

And that raise they offered you? That's actually an advance on your future pay raises. And why are they willing to give you a raise, anyway? Either they must have known that you were underpaid and now they figure that now is the time to give you what you're worth, or you're going to lose out on future income. Either way, they don't have a special fund called "Money for employees we need to convince to stay." My friend and colleague Kristen Henmueller found this out.

You Always Pay for the Counteroffer
by Kristen Henmueller

When I told my boss I was resigning, she turned white. As the only web designer at a large retail operation, with more than ten years of experience with the company, they couldn't lose my knowledge and experience. She asked what the new company would be paying me, and I told her. Later that day, she came back offering me the new salary if I stayed on board.

I liked the company I worked for, and I was comfortable with the work I was doing. Quite frankly I was a bit terrified of starting a new job. One of the biggest reasons I wanted the change was for the bump in salary. This seemed like the best of both worlds, so I agreed to stay on.

I shouldn't have been surprised when I heard from HR the next day. While they would be able to give me the new salary, my job title and pay grade would be lowered. And although I would be getting the higher salary, it was at the top end of the new, lower pay grade. This would directly impact the potential for raises I would have in the future. With a sinking feeling, I realized I shouldn't have taken the offer. Fortunately, I quickly found a third job, and this time I stuck to my guns.

Kristen was lucky here. How much do you want to bet that Kristen would have been let go once her department's crunch time was over? What kind of relationship could she have expected with her boss?

Don't give into the temptation to go back to the job you're comfortable with for more money. Decline the counteroffer.

Be Well Remembered

Once you've given your resignation, your goal until you leave the company is to be well remembered. You want people to say "Ol' Steve, he was a good guy." Leave graciously, and burn no bridges.

No matter how much you may enjoy the thought of telling your boss just how stupid he is, how poorly he runs the department, and how you can't

Don't go out in a blaze of "glory."

wait to hear how they'll manage without you, keep it as a thought. There's no good outcome of your actions, and they can only hurt you. Sending a long, rambling email telling your soon-to-be-ex co-workers about how you're glad to be leaving is pointless and destructive.

People have long memories. We work in an extremely well-connected industry. Send a letter complaining about how terrible the company is, and that's how you'll be remembered. Everything good you've done will be eclipsed by your noisy departure. Chances are it will get around.

Spend your remaining time at the company working on relationships you want to maintain after you're gone. Get contacts and home email addresses for the people who can help you, and who you can help, in your future travels.

Avoid the Exit Interview

At many companies, when you leave you'll stop by HR to take part in an exit interview. You'll typically be asked questions, either verbally or in a questionnaire, about your departure, how you were treated, and what the company could do to improve. It's presented as a way to get things off your chest, to let management know how you really feel, and to unload.

Don't do it. You have nothing to gain by going through this process and can only lose.

First, expect that everything you say will get back to the people you're discussing. Your exit interview is in effect the same thing as telling off your boss, which I just counseled against. You may be promised that the information will be kept confidential, but someone besides the HR clerk has to see it, right? Even if it's not direct information, it's not too hard to figure out where negative comments came from. When you tell HR that your now-ex boss takes a lot of long lunches and is terrible at running meetings, and a few weeks later she comes under scrutiny for those things, it's easy to connect the dots.

Second, if you find yourself wondering "Why are they asking me this *now*, when I'm leaving?" you're on to something. The time to discuss these issues is long past. If you're leaving because, for example, your boss has no interest in helping you with your career, it does you no good to complain about it now. That ship has sailed.

So, what do you say at the exit interview? Simply say, "I don't have any comments to make," and leave it at that.

If you're waiting for the exit interview so that you can say good things about someone at the company or how things are run, then do so directly. Write a letter or email, or tell the persons directly, expressing your gratitude and appreciation for what they've done and how you've appreciated it. This is core to maintaining a healthy network of contacts.

For more about exit interviews, and the potential legal risks, read Nick Corcodilos' article "Exit Interview, Stage Right."[1]

11.7 Getting Rejected

Rejections happen. Despite your best research, a stellar résumé, a wonderful interview, and fantastic references, you're going to get word back that you didn't get the job you wanted. If it's after a first interview, you may get a form letter from the HR department saying "We've decided to go to in a different direction filling this position." If it's after a second or third interview, you'll typically hear back from the hiring manager directly.

I won't pretend that rejection doesn't suck. At the very least, it's disappointing, even if you figured you weren't that interested in the job anyway. It can hurt your feelings, too, and that's OK, because, hey, you're human. Business is business, but you're not a robot.

For what it's worth, it's no picnic for the person doing the rejecting. Only the coldest, most jaded hiring manager isn't bothered by turning down candidates. Even if the person is a lousy candidate and entirely unpleasant, it's no fun calling up to say "Sorry, but no."

---

1. http://www.asktheheadhunter.com/haexit.htm

Rejection Whittles Down the Options

Getting turned down can be the best thing that happens to you on your job hunt, because it's one job eliminated from the field of contenders that is, by definition, not the right job for you.

Remember that a job is a relationship. Both parties have to want the relationship to work in order for the relationship to be a successful, satisfying one. If one party doesn't want the relationship, then it's not going to work. As frustrating as it is to be told "no," at least it's one fewer possibility to have consider.

Get the Most Out of Rejection

It's often possible to get something good out of the situation, however, by asking the hiring manager for advice. You may gain contacts and may even find out what specifically was lacking that knocked you out of the running. You just need to be very careful with your contact at the company, who will be uncomfortable at the time, since he's just had to turn you down for a job.

At some point after the rejection, either at the time of the rejection or a day or two later if it's not comfortable at the time of rejection, ask the person rejecting you for some help. Let's say that the hiring manager has called you up to give the bad news. Your conversation might go something like this.

Manager: *Bob, thanks for the time you've spent coming to meet us. After this round of interviews, we've decided to go with another candidate for the position.*

You: *Thanks for calling me, Tim. Of course I'm disappointed, because Yoyodyne seems like a great place to work, and I enjoyed meeting with Julie and Marsee. It sounds like you've got the right candidate, though, so I'm glad that's worked out for you.*

Note how you're expressing disappointment, in effect reiterating "I do want the job" and helping make the manager more at ease. You're helping him breathe easier and diffusing the tension. This ought to let him open up a bit.

At this point, having done the dirty deed of rejecting you, the manager may want to hang up quickly ("Well, thanks again for your interest." *<click>*) or may be conversational and open to your questions. If it feels like the latter, you can try to tactfully and carefully probe a little to find out what the other candidates had that you didn't or what made them a better fit. Note that you are *not* asking "Why didn't you pick me?" or "What was wrong with me?" or even "What skills was I missing?" Those are questions that are inherently negative, making them harder to answer. Instead, make them positives, without getting personal. Also, do not ask who got the job, because that's none of your business.

Manager: *Yes, I think the choice we're leaning toward is going to work out well. You were in our top three, though.*

You: *Thanks, I'm glad to hear that. If I could ask, what gave the winning candidate the edge?*

Manager: *Well, there were a lot of things. The big one was Oracle. As you know we do a lot with Oracle, and although your SQL knowledge in MySQL was strong, we just felt better with someone with more background in Oracle specifically.*

You: *Absolutely, I can understand that.*

Note that you absolutely are *not* disagreeing or arguing over the decision.[2] Absolutely do not argue with the information you've just been given. Do not try to convince the interviewer that you could learn Oracle if you were just given the chance. The choice has been made, and you must respect it, even if you'd rather have it another way or even if you think the choice was made on faulty assumptions. To do otherwise is extremely disrespectful and makes you look like a whiner. It gives you the stink of desperation.

Now, you can ask for advice and guidance. People like to help other people but don't like to be asked to be given something, so walk the careful line between the two. Ask for guidance in your further path.

You: *Knowing what you know about me and my background, do you have any advice on how I might advance in the future?*

Manager: *Not a lot. I liked what I saw, but this other candidate was just a better fit. Some more up-to-date Java knowledge might*

---

2.   Similarly, this is the same approach to take with getting fired.

help. There are some amazing things happening in on the Apache Tomcat project that you might want to take a look at.

You: *Thanks for that, I'm making a note of it. I appreciate you taking the time to talk to me today. Good luck!*

If you feel that you have built up some sort of rapport with the hiring manager or where you've come in for a second interview but didn't make the final cut, ask for a referral somewhere else. You can ask, "Do you know of any other companies that might make use of my skills?" If you're a good candidate but not right for that job, the hiring manager may help by referring you to another company. She helps herself and her network by sending a qualified candidate to a colleague.

Be careful that you don't come across as pushy or sounding like you're owed something. You're asking for a favor, one of a pointer to another company. You don't want to sound like you're saying "Can you get me a job somewhere else?"

11.8 And the Cycle of Work Continues...

We've walked through the hiring process from head to tail. We've covered everything you should need to get and land a job you love and how to move forward to your next job. Going through this process is always time-consuming and usually more than a little stressful. It's one of those parts of life where you can look back and say "I'm glad that's over with."

But it's never over.

No matter how great your new job is, you're going to need another one again in the future. Nobody stays at their job forever these days. Knowing that, you can optimize your working life and career now to make the next time easier. That's what the final chapter is about.

Chapter 12

Staying Hirable

So you have a good job. You've gone through the hunting and the résumés and the interviews and the references and finally, finally, you've landed the job you want at a company you've always wanted to work for. You can finally relax and forget about the tiring job search.

Sure, put the job search out of your head for a few weeks, maybe a month. Put yourself 110 percent into starting out on the good foot and making a splash at your new gig. And then put your job hunting hat back on. Preparing for the next job is what this chapter is about.

"But I love my new job!" I hear you say. "I just went through this book about getting hired, and now you tell me to plan for my *next* job?" Indeed I am.

Unless you're nearing retirement, you'll be changing employers in the future. No matter how much you love your new job, can you actually see yourself staying at the same company for the rest of your working life? Even if you *can* imagine such a future, it's not entirely in your control.

You can get the rug pulled out from you in a number of ways, none of which you can control. Consider this short list of scenarios that can change your view of your job, if not have you on the street against your will:

- Your boss decides that all programming is going to be done in Java from now on, and you'd rather have a tooth pulled than write Java.

- The company outsources the work your department is doing.

- Your boss is replaced by someone you can't stand.

- A new vice president of IT comes in and decides to "clean house," starting with your department.

- The company decides to move to new headquarters that make your commute unbearable, or even to another state.

- Someone has it in for you and manages to get you fired for some petty offense, or your performance isn't what you thought it was and you're let go.

- A massive recession spurred by the collapse of the banking and automotive industries also causes your company's sales to drop significantly, and you get caught in across-the-board layoffs.

Your need for another job is a "when," not an "if." And since you know that you're going to need another job in the future, you might as well get started on it right now.

Internalize the need to take care of your career, your future jobs, and yourself. It's your responsibility, and no one else's. Please don't fall into the trap of thinking that your employer will take care of your career planning or that your "career path" at work is necessarily what's best for you. Many organizations have career advancement programs, where employees can work to make a career path for their future advancement, and if they do, that's great. However, consider that the company will be aiming your career advancement in a way that ultimately benefits the company best. That may or may not be what's best for you and your career.

> No matter your current job, you're working for yourself.

No matter what your current job is, you're working for yourself. Consider yourself as working for You And Your Family, Inc., and you're a contractor to whomever your current employer is.

The three steps to keeping yourself hirable are these: improve yourself, improve your network, and improve your brand.

12.1 Improve Yourself

Anyone in a technical capacity, from programmer to system administrator to project manager to graphic designer, is in an industry that is constantly innovating and constantly adding new features and capabilities to the world around us. If you're not learning something new, you're falling behind the competition. You may not have the competition now, but you will when that next job comes along.

I'm sure that you understand much of this, because I know you're willing and able to improve yourself. That you are reading this book proves it. If you knew everything and if you thought you were the best you could be and had nothing new to learn, you wouldn't waste your time reading these words.

This self-improvement is not cheap. Some paths to self-improvement will take more time than others, and some may cost money. As with most things in life, you'll get more out when you put more in. Just remember that your investment pays dividends, often right away. Maybe you'll find out about a new project-tracking system or application framework that you can use in your current job. When you're working at improving yourself, people notice as well. This helps improve your branding at work, as I'll discuss in Section 12.3, *Improve Your Brand*, on page 226.

When I talk about self-improvement at conferences, I'll often get someone protesting "But my boss doesn't give us any time to work on side projects" or "We're not Google, and we don't get one day a week to work on side projects!" That's the case for most IT folks, and still people manage to improve their skills. You're the only one in charge of your career, and complaining "I never was given a chance to improve myself" is cold comfort when your skills are out-of-date and you can't get the job you want.

Jump-Start Your Self-improvement

These exercises and activities will help you improve your skills. Each includes a writing, helping, or teaching component, for two reasons.

Teaching is the best way to understand a topic.

First, one of the best ways to improve your learning is by teaching it to someone else. The expectation that we'll be teaching someone else improves our comprehension and retention. We think more about what it is that we've been reading or learning.

Second, writing is a crucial skill that everyone can do a better job at. Think about how much of your communication with others is written text. The importance of being able to use the written word has never been greater.

- Start a blog. See Section 12.3, *Build an Online Presence*, on page 228 for details.

- Join a mailing list for discussion of a technical topic of interest to you, preferably one that is new to you. Better still, create one of your own. Yahoo! Groups[1] and Google Groups[2] let you create one for free in seconds. Get a dozen of your friends and colleagues to join to get things going.

- Learn a new programming language. Write a small but meaningful program with it. Use features not available in your language of choice. What don't you like about the new language? Think about why that feature exists. Write about it.

- Install a new OS. Is it better or worse than your OS of choice? Why are the differences from your current OS there? What makes things easier? Write about it.

- Follow a new blog. Read the previous twenty or thirty entries. Is the author brilliant or full of crap? How does her writing style change? What can you learn about improving your own blog? Pick a great entry, link to it, and write about it.

- Install a new software package or program for your desktop. Think about what you like and don't like about it. Think about how you'd improve it. Think about what ideas you can use yourself. Write about it.

---

1. http://groups.yahoo.com
2. http://groups.google.com

- Join a new technical mailing list or message board. Lurk and listen before posting, trying to absorb the culture. What do you think of individual members? Are they people you'd like to work with? Why or why not? Write about it, without getting too negative and without calling out specific people.

- Join a mailing list or message board related to your customers' interests. If you work for a distributor to restaurants, find a message board for restaurant owners and management. Lurk silently. Resist the temptation to defend your company when it gets bad-mouthed. Listen and think about what you can do to improve things for customers. Write about it.

- Subscribe to a business magazine like *Forbes*, *Business Week*, or *Inc*. Find at least one article that pertains to your company's business. Tear it out, and pass it around the department. Write about it. Read the ads, which are a fascinating window into a culture. Find one that amuses or horrifies you. Write about it.

- Read a new book on a job or industry radically different from what you know. Try to understand the surrounding culture. It could be mortgage risk analysis, police dog training, silversmithing, child care, textile production, or forestry. What are the similarities to your job and industry? What lessons can you take away? Write about them.

- Check out a recorded book from your library, and listen to it on your daily commute. Business books are good, but history is filled with lessons and problems amazingly similar to our life today. The next time you feel frustrated about management at work, listen to a military history, and hear how your company's leadership could be better or much worse. Write about it.

- Take a class. Your local community college probably has something to offer you in a class you can attend once or twice a week at night after work and at a relatively inexpensive cost. Pick something that will help you during the day at work, or pick something that you'd always wanted to learn about but never had a chance to. Write about it.

- Help your children with their homework. What did you forget since you were in school? What are they learning that you never did? What are they learning different from what you learned? Write about it.

- Stretch out at work. Take on a project that requires you to jump in and learn something new. Maybe it won't be a project officially assigned to you, but that still has benefit for you, your department, or your company. Write about it.

- Read. Read. Read. Read as much as you can about as many different things as you can. Then write about it.

Use Your Résumé as a Tracking Tool

Aim to have something interesting to add to your résumé every three months, or every six months at the most. It doesn't have to be a new title or promotion, but your job should be challenging and different enough that you're not doing the same stuff for half a year. It might be a new job responsibility or a new project. Maybe you put together some new system that saved the department a few hours a week in tracking time. Whatever it is, if it provided value to the company, it's résumé-worthy. If it improves who you are as an employee, it's also résumé-worthy.

> If you can't add anything to your résumé semi-annually, you're in a rut.

The résumé rule isn't absolute, but it's a relative indicator. If you're not able to add anything to your résumé, chances are that you're stuck in a career rut. Your skills are probably getting rusty, and it's imperative that you take care of the self-improvement on your own. You may also want to reevaluate the job you're in. If you've done nothing résumé-worthy in six months, are you getting enough challenge to make you excited to go to work? Only you can answer, but use the résumé rule as your first warning flag.

However you get your self-improvement, whether from work or outside (or both!), keep track of it so you can see your own progress. You may not want to bother noting on your résumé that you finished a semester class in ancient Greek history,[3]

---

3. Although you certainly would if it were an accounting class.

but remember it yourself, and feel good about what you've done. And then go do something else. Lather, rinse, repeat.

12.2 Improve Your Network

As I discussed in Section 5.2, *Where the Jobs Are*, on page 84, other people are the most helpful tool you have to finding your next job. Maintaining a solid network of contacts, of people who are willing to help you out, may be as important as any other area of self-improvement. You might have the best skills, but they're not much good if you can't find the job you want. A good network will help you find the job you want and sometimes even get hired.

Your skills and personality may win you the job once you interview, but you have to get the interview in the first place. Having a rich set of contacts is twice as likely to get you that interview

> Getting a job is about who you know *and* what you know.

than any other approach. (Refer to the study in Section 5.2, *The Hard Numbers on Job Boards*, on page 88 for the math.)

That foot in the door is no guarantee of a job, of course. No company worth working for is going to hire someone simply because of who the candidate knows. However, for the hiring manager, the value of a recommendation from a trusted colleague is huge. All other things being equal, I'm going to want to hire someone recommended by someone I trust before I get someone green from the streets.

Your contacts are real people who know you. They know that helping someone else is a great way to get helped yourself later. Your business contacts need not be what you would call "friends," people you would go have a beer with, to provide you value. Your colleague may just be someone you've done work with, or worked for, and you have a valuable business relationship.

Building a Network

It should be clear by now that people are crucial to ongoing career choices. They lead you to the good jobs and help you get them. Having a large, varied network of people who know and trust you may well be the number-one determinant of what options and jobs you have available to you in the future.

You get part of your network by default. People you've gone to school with, or worked with in recent years, are the core of your business network. Family members as well are excellent contacts when it comes time to look for a new job in earnest.

This core of contacts is not enough, however. Everyone else has co-workers, school alumni, and family members to help. You want a bigger, more helpful network than the other guy. You also want to meet new people and have new contacts. Your co-workers, family, and school friends are all based in the past. Building a network is about moving into the future.

"That's great, Andy," I hear you say, "but I'm not a social kind of person. I'm not very outgoing, and I don't have time to work on that." I understand that concern. I wasn't always outgoing, either. I can only ask "Can you afford *not* to expand your network?"

I'm not suggesting that you change who you are but rather how you view others around you. The rest of the world isn't a nuisance but rather a source of new experiences, new backgrounds, and probably more than a few new friends, if you'll allow yourself to find them. From a mercenary point of view, it's also a source of new business contacts who will help you find and land your next great job.

Simple Ways to Improve Your Network

Here are simple, concrete ways to help improve your social network. Some are direct, some indirect, but all help you get into the way of thinking about social contacts that will be standard in the coming years. Note that in some cases, the activities overlap with those already discussed in Section 12.1, *Jump-Start Your Self-improvement*, on page 217.

- Have lunch with someone outside your department. Surely there are people in your company whom you are acquainted with, but not that well. Aim for once a week.

- Go to a user group meeting in your area of expertise. The group may be technical or purely social. Either way, meet as many people as you can. Find out about others, and let them know about you. Then look at user groups in areas you don't know but would like to know.

- Join a new mailing list in your area of expertise. Answer technical questions. *Follow up* with those you've helped to see whether your advice did the trick. You're far more likely to make a connection with that person.

- Go to a meeting or join a mailing list about something non-technical that interests you. Maybe you raise tropical fish, so join a tropical fish group. People you know outside of a business capacity can still turn into technical contacts.

- Hang out in an IRC channel related to your area of expertise. Answer questions. Try a channel on a topic you'd like to know more about.

- Send mail to someone whose work you admired or wrote a blog post you learned from.

- Send an instant message to someone whose work you admired, if they publish their address. More and more people are using Jabber, AIM, Yahoo! Messenger, and the like, and this can be an easy way to introduce yourself to someone without the fear of meeting face-to-face.

- Thank the manager at a restaurant for a great meal or great service from the wait staff. It's the opposite of what they've come to expect. It's also great practice for learning to say "I like X, and I thank you for it."

- Learn to shake hands with confidence. In the United States, shaking hands is a universal gesture of business greeting, whether the parties are male, female, or both. The tactile feedback of hand against hand also helps drop your mental defenses and makes you more open to talking to the other person. See the sidebar on page 144 for more.

Clearly, some of these will have you meet more new people than others. Some, like having lunch with different people, are habits you get into, where others, like going to user groups, take more practice. All will help build your social circle and make you more comfortable with meeting people.

Make It Easier to Meet Other People

For some of you, this level of social interaction may be intimidating. Our industry attracts those who enjoy working with machines and may less enjoy the human aspects. That's not at all an indictment but an observation. That said, it's still important to have a network that involves real live people to help you in your career.

Before you go down this road, take a look at how you see others. Are you a comparer, silently measuring your value against the value of others? If so, know that it is toxic to your happiness and your career. There is no surer way to scuttle existing relationships and inhibit the growth of new ones.

The Internet has done away with the face-to-face caste systems that used to keep people stratified. People who you might see as "above," you are just the same as you and everyone else. They're not imbued with special powers, and they probably don't have the attitude that you are not worthy of social interaction with them. If they do, it's a character flaw in *who* they are, not *what* they've achieved.

> Industry rock stars are just regular people.

This means that the people you admire, or even idolize, are not in some imagined ivory tower to be watched from afar. Indeed, they are potentially some of the greatest contacts you can have. Whether in person or in email and whether at work, at a meeting, or a conference, you have no reason not to meet the people who you admire.

The easiest way to get to meet someone you see as "above" you is to tell him or her "Hi, I'm Bob Smith. I like what you did, and I thank you for it." It could be in email, or it could be in person, but it always starts simple. The first time I met Dave Thomas, one of the publishers of this very book, I recognized him in an elevator at a conference and told him I loved the book he cowrote, *The Pragmatic Programmer* [HT00], and that I was glad the book existed for me to refer newer programmers to.

This approach works for a number of reasons. First, it gives you something to say and some common ground. You're both familiar with what the person has done, so you can both intelligently discuss it if the person chooses to. Second, it puts the person

Can Facebook Get Me a Job?

In recent years, sites like Facebook, LinkedIn, and Twitter have made social networking a game. It's fun to search for people you know and add them to your list of friends or contacts. In a way, it's social networking, but not like I'm talking about here.

The sort of network I'm talking about is of colleagues, of people who can and will help you in your career, and for whom you'd return the favor. Keeping track of these folks on LinkedIn may help keep them in front of mind, but what good is having 200 contacts on a site if they're not there in a pinch?

I'm not at all bashing any of these sites. I have plenty of contacts on all three and will likely have plenty more on the dozens of others that pop up after this book is printed. Just don't confuse someone you only vaguely know because they friended you on Facebook with someone who's looking out for you.

you're talking with in a positive frame of mind. Everyone likes having their work admired and appreciated.

Try it next time you go to a user group meeting where someone gives a talk. If you liked the talk, just say that. "Hi, I'm Bob Smith. Thanks for the talk. I liked what you were saying about backup strategies." Even if it wasn't all that fascinating, you probably learned *something*, right? You can say "Hi, I'm Bob Smith. Some of those software packages I'd never heard of before. Thanks for speaking tonight."

Do not criticize the person you're meeting, because that's how you'll be remembered. If you go up and say "Yeah, hi, I just wanted to tell you that you spelled *accessory* wrong on slide 12," you'll be remembered as the person who complained about the slides.

Of course, all these same ideas apply when you're emailing or IMing someone. "I like what you did, and I appreciate it." As with face-to-face discussions, it's respectful and it leaves the door open for more conversation, if the person wants it.

Keeping Track of Your Contacts

As you build your social network, keep track of who they are, and their vital information. Keep a database of your contacts, with scraps of information to help you remember who people are and how you know them. Not only is that person your contact, you are also his or hers. Tracking these tidbits of information will help you down the road when you get an email from someone you only somewhat remember. "Aha!" you'll exclaim, "she was that artist from Indiana I met at a web conference a few years ago."

Tracking contacts doesn't have to be fancy, and you don't need some big fancy-shmancy contact database designed for a sales person. You can use Outlook on Windows, or you can use Address Book on the Mac. There are any number of options available to you out on the Net, of course. You can track everything in a text file if it works for you.

The information doesn't have to be detailed. Track email addresses and phone numbers if you have them, of course, but that's just what it takes to get in touch with someone. I like to track business specifics, like where the person works and what his or her title is. Web page and blog URLs fit along these lines. It's also good to note personal things if they come up, like a spouse's name or names and ages of children. Then, in notes fields, I add specifics of the reason for knowing this person. It might be a project name or a conference where you met, but it should be enough to help you remember if that person comes out of the dark past and you've forgotten the connection.

This tracking of information must become a habit, or it won't get done. You can't slack off for years and then decide you'd better hurry up and write everything down because your job is in jeopardy. The only way to build your network, and the database of information about the people in it, is to cultivate it continually over time, as a habit.

12.3 Improve Your Brand

Your brand is crucial in your job search and in your day-to-day life at work. Before you sneer at the word *brand* as being "marketing," consider the power of the concept of the brand.

Brands are all around us in the real world. What do you think of when you hear the name Microsoft? Walmart? America Online? Apple? Some you love, some you hate. Many people are their own brands: Oprah, Tom Cruise, Matt Groening, Elvis, Bono, and David Letterman, for example. Again, some you love, some you hate.

It's not just celebrities who have strong brands. In our own industry, we have Bill Gates, Richard Stallman, Steve Jobs, Steve McConnell, Bill Joy, Larry Wall, and Steve Ballmer. Each of these probably conjures up an image and reaction for you.

The fact is, everyone has a brand, whether he wants it or not. Whether it's a good or bad brand, and what you do with it, is up to you.

> You have a brand, whether you want it or not.

A colleague of mine, active in the Perl community, once told of interviewing for a Perl job. The hiring manager explained right off "My guys all know your work. We don't need to discuss your technical background." What a reputation to have, to have your technical *bona fides* not questioned at a job interview! That's the power of a strong brand.

Brand is just shorthand for your reputation, how you're known, and what people think of you. I specifically use the word *brand* because it is a business term, and you're doing work to help business. Let the business angle help shape your thinking.

At work, your brand works for you and against you. It affects how you're seen by everyone around you, even if they haven't met you. It affects the projects you get assigned to and how much money you get when it's time for raises.

How are you seen at work? Which of these words applies to how others see you?

- Helpful? Or obstructive?
- Diligent? Or lazy?
- Approachable? Or standoffish?
- Careful? Or sloppy?
- Humble? Or arrogant?
- Attentive? Or careless?
- Eager? Or apathetic?

Perception is reality.

Are you sure? Be honest with yourself, because it doesn't matter what your perception is as much as the perceptions of others. You may think you're the nicest guy in the place, but if you're the only one who sees it that way, then it doesn't much matter.

A brand is also based on the work you do. If the projects you're working on are cutting edge, that reflects on you. If you never do more than rote reporting applications, chances are people around the company won't remember you. Your brand is also what people see each day in the results you produce. Are you someone who consistently turns out good work, who makes things run smoothly, and who brings projects in on time? Or are you the guy who blows Monday mornings and Friday afternoons reading Slashdot? Are you sure?

For more on personal branding, please pick up a copy of Tom Peters' excellent *The Brand You 50* [Pet99].

Build an Online Presence

If you're serious about your personal brand, you need an online presence that supports your personal brand now and in the future. Maintaining your online presence is important to giving a proper impression to your future employers.

I'm not talking about a big fancy website. At the very least, you should have a blog or some place where you can be found by name and where you show off your technical skill. A blog is likely the first hit that a potential employer will find when doing a web search for you. You want that to represent at least some of your professional skills.

If you already have a blog, or a personal website, but it's not technical, start a technical one. Keep it separate from the personal blog. A future employer won't be inspired to call you for an interview by your trip to the Grand Canyon. What I'm talking about is a tech-related blog that just deals with what value you have to an employer. For those who don't, start a blog today.

Your blog need not be complicated, and it can be almost trivial to create. You can create one through Blogger[4] or WordPress[5] for free in a matter of minutes.

Treat your blog like a technical diary. Use it to reflect on the work you've done over time, as you do it. Populate it with information that will give employers a sense of your technical skills, as well as a running journal of day-to-day activities.

For example, one day you might write this:

> **You, in your blog:** *Spent half a day playing with LogFoo today. It's a new open source website log analysis tool I saw mentioned on Slashdot, and the sample reports were impressive. We've been using WebBonker for over two years now, and I figure it wouldn't hurt to look around.*
>
> *Unfortunately, it wasn't a good experience. Installation was a chore. There wasn't a prebuilt RPM package for it, so I had to install a half dozen dependent libraries on a scratch server, and then spent a good hour monkeying with configuration parameters just to get it to install.*
>
> *Finally, when I got it going, it was slooooow. It took more than an hour to analyze the last year of logs from the website. And then, when it finally generated the reports, they were these bland reports, nothing like the demo. Turns out the demo reports require the Stylizer add-on and some style pack. What a pain.*

That's not so tough to write. It may take you ten or twenty minutes, but the investment will last for years. It's like putting away money in a special account with each paycheck. Blog just twice a month, and in a year you've got twenty-four entries that give potential employers insight into your skills and background better than any résumé can.

Your blog can be more powerful than any résumé.

---

4. http://www.blogger.com/
5. http://wordpress.com/

Blog about anything you've done that you might tell a techie buddy about at lunch or over beers after work. Make sure that you're not just reporting like it's a news story but that you tell something about you at the same time.

Here are some ideas to get you thinking. Note how each one sounds like it might be a story you'd tell at an interview.

- A particularly pernicious bug you found in some code and how you fixed it
- The story of a terrible catastrophe, how you fixed it, and how you helped prevent it from happening again
- An article about software development methodology and your opinions about what it said
- Your five favorite books about Linux
- The three Photoshop filters you use most, and why
- Your experience trying out a new editor, or programming language, or some other tool
- What you'd like to change in your current editor/language/tool

Don't worry if people aren't going to read it. This is for your benefit, mostly. It's your career journal—your running log of what you've done and why you rock.

However, there's tangible value besides to you. Chances are that you'll get some contacts. Someone searching the Web for the same cryptic error message you were stumped by will find your blog entry, where she'll learn what you did to solve the problem. That person may also contact you to thank you and become a member of your technical network. You never know what will happen.

Remember, chance favors the prepared mind, as well as the blogger who publishes good content.

12.4 Always Look for Your Next Job

You know you'll need another job some day. You know you'll need to be prepared when that day comes. There's no better way to keep this mind-set than to always have your eyes open for your next great job.

Do some low-key searching of job sites every so often. Sign up for a local job listing mailing list. Subscribe to the RSS feed for a bulletin board that specializes in your area of expertise. This will keep a steady stream of job information passing in front of you. Maybe 95 percent of it is uninteresting, but that other 5 percent could be gold.

None of this is to say that you should pursue the jobs that you spy. Don't pursue an alternative job just because something comes by that you're qualified for. However, do take the time to consider what you see. Think about the trade-offs you'd make, and assess your current situation.

There Could Be Something Better

Even the best jobs might be eclipsed by another opportunity, but you won't know unless you're looking for them. Consider the possibilities:

- Opportunity to lead a new team on a groundbreaking project.
- Working in an industry that's always fascinated you
- Working for a company whose products you love (I once pursued a sysadmin position working for Touch & Go Records, while a friend flirted with a job with his beloved Chicago Cubs.)
- A chance to work someplace you've wanted to move to, whether another part of the country, or another country altogether.
- A job working with someone whom you've always admired
- Significantly higher pay for a similar position

If you close off the idea that there could be a situation even better for you than your current job, even if you're perfectly happy, you could be missing a great opportunity.

Looking Helps You Prepare

Whether the next job you pursue is because an excellent opportunity falls in your lap or because you're unceremoniously out on the street, being prepared will make it easier when the time comes. It may save precious time when you need to strike.

Could you apply for a job tomorrow if you needed to?

How ready are you to apply for a new job? Whether because of a loss of a current job or finding an excellent new opportunity that needs to be acted on quickly, consider how many of these apply to you right now:

- Your résumé is up-to-date.

- Your skills are competitive with the rest of the job market.

- You have at least five people you could turn to help you find your next job.

- You have at least three references who can speak to your work ability.

Looking for your next job helps keep these at front of mind so that when the time comes, you're ready.

Looking Keeps You Smart

Looking for your next job helps you get a feel for the industry in your region. If all you think about from day-to-day is your job, your little niche of the computer business, you'll miss everything else going on around you. Keeping the blinders off is the only way to see what's available.

Try this: this Sunday, grab a newspaper for your nearest big city, and spread out to read the classifieds. Read every computer-related ad. Mark the jobs that seem interesting. Note the ones that you could tolerate if you had to in a pinch. Marvel at how you're completely unqualified for many of them. Look for terms you don't understand and for positions you haven't heard of. What are SPSS, .NET, SharePoint, Peoplesoft, or Drupal? What's a SAN, and why do you need a SAN administrator to take care of it? Answering these questions will be educational in general and may uncover some new ideas or directions in specific.

When you're done, think about what you knew and what you didn't know. Any trends that surprised you? Looking for your next job will help you stay connected to what's going on.

Looking Helps You Assess Your Current Situation

Perhaps most important, looking at other employment possibilities helps you verify to yourself that the job you're currently in is indeed the best choice for you right now or that you should move on. It can help you feel better about your current job and appreciate what you've got to see what the alternatives are.

The next time you feel yourself grumbling that you're overworked and underpaid, take a look at the alternatives. See what other companies are paying for comparable work. Maybe you're overpaid for the market, and you should be thankful for what you've got. Maybe the low pay isn't because of the company, but because your position and skillset aren't worth as much. Whatever the situation, looking for your next job is the primary research to do.

When you've assessed your situation, you can't help but think about the competition for the next job or for the job you have now. You get a feel for what skills are in demand, which may well turn out to be skills you need. These help inform your direction for self-improvement, as discussed at the beginning of the chapter.

There's Nothing Wrong with Looking

There's nothing at all disloyal about looking for your next job. First, your primary loyalty has to be to yourself, not to your organization. If your employer is not fulfilling the needs that you have (thinking back to Chapter 2, *What Do You Want in a Job?*, on page 19), then it's time to move on. Even if you ignore your own needs, staying in a job where you're not doing your best means you're not giving your best to the company. Eventually, you'll be out anyway.

Second, I guarantee you that your company has no loyalty to you. Your parents or grandparents may wax rhapsodic about how in times past, loyalty **Company loyalty does not exist.** meant something, and your years of service meant that you could have a job for life. Those days are now gone.

For that matter, a company cannot be loyal, because a company is a shifting amalgam of people in a given point in time.

Even something as somewhat definable as "company culture" changes over time. People can be loyal, but organizations cannot. The best someone could promise you is "You'll have a job here as long as I'm around," but what happens when that person leaves or is fired?

I don't mean to sound cold or mercenary, but I don't want anyone to have the delusion that "loyalty" means anything in the relationship between employee and employer. Employees and employers come together to do the best work possible, and they go their separate ways when the situation requires it.

None of us wants to be in the situation where we have to get a new job. Being prepared for that scenario will make things much easier when it comes.

12.5 It's Never the End

We're at the end of this chapter and the end of this book, but it's not the end of your reading. Beyond the idea of staying hirable is the larger subject of career management. I suggest you follow up this book with Chad Fowler's excellent *The Passionate Programmer* [Fow09]. Reading the first edition of that book was one of my inspirations for writing this one.

I hope that you'll see your career as a geek-for-hire as one that always has one more cool program to create, one more feat of network wizardry, or one more excellent hack to pull off. As technical professionals, we are blessed to have the skills to be well paid for jobs that we love. Not just like, but *love*. Please don't settle for anything less.

Meaningless Clichés to Avoid

Corporate jargon isn't the only source of meaningless blather. The following clichés would make an excellent start for Buzz-word Bingo, Résumé Edition.[1]

- Professional.
- Hard worker; efficient; strong work ethic.
- Quick learner; love to learn.
- Strong communication skills.
- Highly motivated; self-starter; makes things happen.
- Dedicated; determined; reliable.
- Good with people; a real people person.
- Eager; aggressive; a real go-getter.
- Team player.
- Customer-focused.
- Problem solver.
- I do whatever it takes to get the job done.

Everyone is "professional" and "dedicated" and a "team player," so these descriptions fail to distinguish you from the crowd. To turn these clunkers into words that matter, see Chapter 3, *Résumé Content: Getting the Words Down*, on page 35.

---

1. Never seen Buzzword Bingo? See mine at http://theworkinggeek.com/bingo/.

Résumé, Cover Letter, and Email Killers

The written word is how most of us communicate in our industry. Being able to write is a minimum for entry, not a skill. Read Chapter 3, *Résumé Content: Getting the Words Down*, on page 35; Chapter 4, *Building Your Résumé Documents*, on page 65; and Section 6.2, *Create a Cover Letter*, on page 112.

- Spelling errors
- Sloppy production
- Too much document, too little content
- Errors about people, such as misspelling someone's name or confusing his or her gender
- Having a silly email address like packers_fan_497 @gmail.com or live_for_beer@hotmail.com
- Not following directions, such as sending a PDF instead of a Word document
- Speaking ill of anyone, especially current or past employers
- Fluff words and meaningless clichés (see Appendix A, on page 235, for more info)
- Personal information, especially anything discriminatory (see Chapter 10, *Too Much Information*, on page 183)
- Too much talk of your needs, not the employer's

Appendix C

Interview Killers

Any of these during an interview will weigh heavily against you, if not end the interview abruptly. For more on the right and wrong of interviewing, see Chapter 8, *The Interview*, on page 139.

- Showing up late
- Being unprepared
- Chewing gum or smoking, or smelling like smoke
- Using a limp handshake
- Have bad breath or body odor
- Coming underdressed or sloppily dressed
- Speaking ill of anyone, especially current or past employers
- Complaining, or discussing your problems
- Bringing up money, benefits, sick days, and so on
- Appearing disinterested or aloof
- Not asking questions of your own
- Appearing overenthusiastic or desperate
- Lying
- Leaving your phone on
- Having to cut the interview short

Appendix D

Web Resources

Land the Tech Job You Love home page...

... http://pragprog.com/titles/algh/

The source for updates and information about this book, plus an online discussion forum to share with other readers.

The Working Geek .... http://theworkinggeek.com

The author's blog about working life for the technical professional, including the job hunt and beyond.

Ask The Headhunter .... http://asktheheadhunter.com

Nick Corcodilos' companion website to his inspiring book _Ask the Headhunter_ [Cor97].

Appendix E

Bibliography

[BJ82]   Kenneth Blanchard and Spencer Johnson. *The One Minute Manager*. Berkeley Publishing Group, New York, 1982.

[Con05]   Damian Conway. *Perl Best Practices*. O'Reilly Media, Inc., Sebastopol, CA, 2005.

[Cor97]   Nick Corcodilos. *Ask the Headhunter: Reinventing the Interview to Win the Job*. Plume, New York, 1997.

[DR08]   Margaret Riley Dikel and Frances E. Roehm. *Guide To Internet Job Searching 2008–2009*. McGraw-Hill, New York, 2008.

[Fow09]   Chad Fowler. *The Passionate Programmer: Creating a Remarkable Career in Software Development*. The Pragmatic Programmers, LLC, Raleigh, NC, and Dallas, TX, 2009.

[HT00]   Andrew Hunt and David Thomas. *The Pragmatic Programmer: From Journeyman to Master*. Addison-Wesley, Reading, MA, 2000.

[Lim06]   Thomas A. Limoncelli. *Time Management For System Administrators*. O'Reilly Media, Inc., Sebastopol, CA, 2006.

[McC04]   Steve McConnell. *Code Complete: A Practical Hand-book of Software Construction*. Microsoft Press, Red-mond, WA, 2004.

[Pet99]   Tom Peters. *The Brand You 50: Fifty Ways to Trans-form Yourself from an "Employee" into a Brand That Shouts Distinction, Commitment, and Passion!* Alfred A. Knopf, Inc, New York, 1999.

[RD05]   Johanna Rothman and Esther Derby. *Behind Closed Doors: Secrets of Great Management*. The Pragmatic Programmers, LLC, Raleigh, NC, and Dallas, TX, 2005.

[Rot04]   Johanna Rothman. *Hiring the Best Knowledge Work-ers, Techies, and Nerds: The Secrets and Science of Hiring Technical People*. Dorset House, New York, 2004.

[SE99]   Stephen Spainhour and Robert Eckstein. *Webmaster In a Nutshell*. O'Reilly & Associates, Inc, Sebastopol, CA, 1999.

Index

The Pragmatic Bookshelf

Available in paperback and DRM-free PDF, our titles are here to help you stay on top of your game. The following are in print as of May 2009; be sure to check our website at pragprog.com for newer titles.

Title	Year	ISBN	Pages
Advanced Rails Recipes: 84 New Ways to Build Stunning Rails Apps	2008	9780978739225	464
Agile Retrospectives: Making Good Teams Great	2006	9780977616640	200
Agile Web Development with Rails, Third Edition	2009	9781934356166	784
Augmented Reality: A Practical Guide	2008	9781934356036	328
Behind Closed Doors: Secrets of Great Management	2005	9780976694021	192
Best of Ruby Quiz	2006	9780976694076	304
Core Animation for Mac OS X and the iPhone: Creating Compelling Dynamic User Interfaces	2008	9781934356104	200
Data Crunching: Solve Everyday Problems using Java, Python, and More	2005	9780974514079	208
Deploying Rails Applications: A Step-by-Step Guide	2008	9780978739201	280
Design Accessible Web Sites: 36 Keys to Creating Content for All Audiences and Platforms	2007	9781934356029	336
Desktop GIS: Mapping the Planet with Open Source Tools	2008	9781934356067	368
Developing Facebook Platform Applications with Rails	2008	9781934356128	200
Enterprise Integration with Ruby	2006	9780976694069	360
Enterprise Recipes with Ruby and Rails	2008	9781934356234	416
Everyday Scripting with Ruby: for Teams, Testers, and You	2007	9780977616619	320
FXRuby: Create Lean and Mean GUIs with Ruby	2008	9781934356074	240
From Java To Ruby: Things Every Manager Should Know	2006	9780976694090	160
GIS for Web Developers: Adding Where to Your Web Applications	2007	9780974514093	275
Google Maps API, V2: Adding Where to Your Applications	2006	PDF-Only	83
Groovy Recipes: Greasing the Wheels of Java	2008	9780978739294	264
Hello, Android: Introducing Google's Mobile Development Platform	2008	9781934356173	200
Interface Oriented Design	2006	9780976694052	240
Learn to Program, 2nd Edition	2009	9781934356364	230

Continued on next page

Title	Year	ISBN	Pages
Manage It! Your Guide to Modern Pragmatic Project Management	2007	9780978739249	360
Mastering Dojo: JavaScript and Ajax Tools for Great Web Experiences	2008	9781934356111	568
No Fluff Just Stuff 2006 Anthology	2006	9780977616664	240
No Fluff Just Stuff 2007 Anthology	2007	9780978739287	320
Practical Programming: An Introduction to Computer Science Using Python	2009	9781934356272	350
Practices of an Agile Developer	2006	9780974514086	208
Pragmatic Project Automation: How to Build, Deploy, and Monitor Java Applications	2004	9780974514031	176
Pragmatic Thinking and Learning: Refactor Your Wetware	2008	9781934356050	288
Pragmatic Unit Testing in C# with NUnit	2007	9780977616671	176
Pragmatic Unit Testing in Java with JUnit	2003	9780974514017	160
Pragmatic Version Control Using Git	2008	9781934356159	200
Pragmatic Version Control using CVS	2003	9780974514000	176
Pragmatic Version Control using Subversion	2006	9780977616657	248
Programming Erlang: Software for a Concurrent World	2007	9781934356005	536
Programming Groovy: Dynamic Productivity for the Java Developer	2008	9781934356098	320
Programming Ruby: The Pragmatic Programmers' Guide, Second Edition	2004	9780974514055	864
Programming Ruby 1.9: The Pragmatic Programmers' Guide	2009	9781934356081	960
Prototype and script.aculo.us: You Never Knew JavaScript Could Do This!	2007	9781934356012	448
Rails Recipes	2006	9780977616602	350
Rails for .NET Developers	2008	9781934356203	300
Rails for Java Developers	2007	9780977616695	336
Rails for PHP Developers	2008	9781934356043	432
Rapid GUI Development with QtRuby	2005	PDF-Only	83
Release It! Design and Deploy Production-Ready Software	2007	9780978739218	368
Scripted GUI Testing with Ruby	2008	9781934356180	192
Ship it! A Practical Guide to Successful Software Projects	2005	9780974514048	224
Stripes ...And Java Web Development Is Fun Again	2008	9781934356210	375
TextMate: Power Editing for the Mac	2007	9780978739232	208
The Definitive ANTLR Reference: Building Domain-Specific Languages	2007	9780978739256	384

Continued on next page

Title	Year	ISBN	Pages
The Passionate Programmer: Creating a Remarkable Career in Software Development	2009	9781934356340	200
ThoughtWorks Anthology	2008	9781934356142	240
Ubuntu Kung Fu: Tips, Tricks, Hints, and Hacks	2008	9781934356227	400

Expand Your Horizons

The Passionate Programmer

This book is about creating a remarkable career in software development. Remarkable careers don't come by chance. They require thought, intention, action, and a willingness to change course when you've made mistakes. Most of us have been stumbling around letting our careers take us where they may. It's time to take control.

This revised and updated second edition lays out a strategy for planning and creating a radically successful life in software development *(the first edition was released as My Job Went to India: 52 Ways To Save Your Job)*.

The Passionate Programmer: Creating a Remarkable Career in Software Development
Chad Fowler
(200 pages) ISBN: 978-1934356-34-0. $23.95
http://pragprog.com/titles/cfcar2

Pragmatic Thinking and Learning

Software development happens in your head. Not in an editor, IDE, or design tool. In this book by Pragmatic Programmer Andy Hunt, you'll learn how our brains are wired, and how to take advantage of your brain's architecture. You'll master new tricks and tips to learn more, faster, and retain more of what you learn.

• Use the Dreyfus Model of Skill Acquisition to become more expert • Leverage the architecture of the brain to strengthen different thinking modes
• Avoid common "known bugs" in your mind
• Learn more deliberately and more effectively
• Manage knowledge more efficiently

Pragmatic Thinking and Learning:
Refactor your Wetware
Andy Hunt
(288 pages) ISBN: 978-1-9343560-5-0. $34.95
http://pragprog.com/titles/ahptl

Mac and iPhone Development

iPhone SDK Development

Jump into application development for today's most remarkable mobile communications platform, the Pragmatic way. This Pragmatic guide takes you through the tools and APIs, the same ones Apple uses for its applications, that you can use to create your own software for the iPhone and iPod touch. Packed with useful examples, this book will give you both the big-picture concepts and the everyday "gotcha" details that developers need to make the most of the beauty and power of the iPhone OS platform.

iPhone SDK Development
Bill Dudney, Chris Adamson, Marcel Molina
(430 pages) ISBN: 978-1-9343562-5-8. $38.95
http://pragprog.com/titles/amiphd

Core Animation for OS X/iPhone

Have you seen Apple's Front Row application and Cover Flow effects? Then you've seen Core Animation at work. It's about making applications that give strong visual feedback through movement and morphing, rather than repainting panels. This comprehensive guide will get you up to speed quickly and take you into the depths of this new technology.

Core Animation for Mac OS X and the iPhone: Creating Compelling Dynamic User Interfaces
Bill Dudney
(220 pages) ISBN: 978-1-9343561-0-4. $34.95
http://pragprog.com/titles/bdcora

Pragmatic Management

Behind Closed Doors

You can learn to be a better manager—even a great manager—with this guide. You'll find powerful tips covering:

- Delegating effectively • Using feedback and goal-setting • Developing influence • Handling one-on-one meetings • Coaching and mentoring • Deciding what work to do-and what not to do • . . . and more!

Behind Closed Doors: Secrets of Great Management
Johanna Rothman and Esther Derby
(192 pages) ISBN: 0-9766940-2-6. $24.95
http://pragprog.com/titles/rdbcd

Manage It!

Manage It! is an award-winning, risk-based guide to making good decisions about how to plan and guide your projects. Author Johanna Rothman shows you how to beg, borrow, and steal from the best methodologies to fit your particular project. You'll find what works best for *you*.

- Learn all about different project lifecycles • See how to organize a project • Compare sample project dashboards • See how to staff a project • Know when you're done—and what that means.

Manage It! Your Guide to Modern, Pragmatic Project Management
Johanna Rothman
(360 pages) ISBN: 0-9787392-4-8. $34.95
http://pragprog.com/titles/jrpm

The Home of Ruby and Rails

Programming Ruby 1.9 (The Pickaxe for 1.9)

The Pickaxe book, named for the tool on the cover, is the definitive reference to this highly-regarded language.

- Up-to-date and expanded for Ruby version 1.9
- Complete documentation of all the built-in classes, modules, and methods • Complete descriptions of all standard libraries • Learn more about Ruby's web tools, unit testing, and programming philosophy

Programming Ruby 1.9: The Pragmatic Programmers' Guide
Dave Thomas with Chad Fowler and Andy Hunt
(992 pages) ISBN: 978-1-9343560-8-1. $49.95
http://pragprog.com/titles/ruby3

Agile Web Development with Rails

Rails is a full-stack, open-source web framework, with integrated support for unit, functional, and integration testing. It enforces good design principles, consistency of code across your team (and across your organization), and proper release management. This is the newly updated Third Edition, which goes beyond the award winning previous editions with new material covering the latest advances in Rails 2.0.

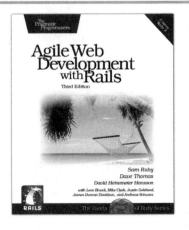

Agile Web Development with Rails: Third Edition
Sam Ruby, Dave Thomas, and David Heinemeier Hansson, et al.
(784 pages) ISBN: 978-1-9343561-6-6. $43.95
http://pragprog.com/titles/rails3

The Pragmatic Bookshelf

The Pragmatic Bookshelf features books written by developers for developers. The titles continue the well-known Pragmatic Programmer style and continue to garner awards and rave reviews. As development gets more and more difficult, the Pragmatic Programmers will be there with more titles and products to help you stay on top of your game.

Visit Us Online

Land the Tech Job You Love's Home Page
http://pragprog.com/titles/algh
Source code from this book, errata, and other resources. Come give us feedback, too!

Register for Updates
http://pragprog.com/updates
Be notified when updates and new books become available.

Join the Community
http://pragprog.com/community
Read our weblogs, join our online discussions, participate in our mailing list, interact with our wiki, and benefit from the experience of other Pragmatic Programmers.

New and Noteworthy
http://pragprog.com/news
Check out the latest pragmatic developments, new titles and other offerings.

Save on the eBook

Save on the eBook versions of this title. Owning the paper version of this book entitles you to purchase the electronic versions at a terrific discount.

PDFs are great for carrying around on your laptop—they are hyperlinked, have color, and are fully searchable. Most titles are also available for the iPhone and iPod touch, Amazon Kindle, and other popular e-book readers.

Buy now at pragprog.com/coupon.

Contact Us

Online Orders:	www.pragprog.com/catalog
Customer Service:	support@pragprog.com
Non-English Versions:	translations@pragprog.com
Pragmatic Teaching:	academic@pragprog.com
Author Proposals:	proposals@pragprog.com
Contact us:	1-800-699-PROG (+1 919 847 3884)